D0531240

2

Jean Nouvel

3

WITHDRAWN

# Jean Nouvel

THE ELEMENTS OF ARCHITECTURE

CONWAY LLOYD MORGAN

 THAMES AND HUDSON

First published in Great Britain in 1998 by Thames
and Hudson Ltd, London

Copyright © 1998 Universe Publishing

British Library Cataloguing-in-Publication Data
A catalogue record for this book is available from
the British Library

ISBN 0-500-28089-4

Printed in Italy

# Contents

# Acknowledgments

This book is for Marc, with love.

I first met Jean Nouvel through the good offices of Laurence King, who invited us to work together on the *International Design Yearbook*. I found the wit, subtlety, and intelligence of his buildings reflected in the man himself. His interest in this project has been inspiring for me, and his time and attention have made working on this book an immense pleasure.

Two other people played an important role in the making of this book. Charlotte Kruk is Nouvel's personal assistant, an elegant fireball of enthusiasm and efficiency. Her help and humor were invaluable. Philippe Ruault, whose photographs are a major part of this book, was always ready to share his opinions on photography, architecture, and architects, particularly if there was a good bottle of Bordeaux to hand. I am very grateful to them both.

My thanks also to the members of Jean Nouvel's team who took time off from busy schedules to discuss present and past projects: Marie-Hélène Baldran, Didier Brault, Henriette Denis, Gunther Domenig, Isabelle Guillauic, Eric Maria, Brigitte Metra Weber, Frédérique Monjanel, Laurent Niget, and Françoise Raynaud.

Other friends and colleagues gave help and advice. I would particularly like to thank Gaston Bergeret, Olivier Boissière, Alain Bonny, Edouard Boucher, Marc Emery, Georges Fessy, Patrice Goulet, Casper Grathwohl, Guillaume Neuhaus, Philippa Pawley, Tom Porter, Hubert Tonka, and Janet Turner. Young-mi Kim, Martin Pawley, Lynda Relph-Knight, and Nico Turner have also encouraged me to write about Nouvel in the past, for which much thanks.

Finally, very special thanks go to Elizabeth Johnson for the wisdom of her editing and her patience with an author on the different side of the Atlantic.

Conway Lloyd Morgan
London, June 1998

# The New Nouvel

Architectures Jean Nouvel was created in 1995, after the collapse of Nouvel's five-year partnership with Emmanuel Cattani. The offices moved at the same time, from a single floor just off the rue Oberkampf in the eleventh arrondisement in Paris to a three-story building at the end of a nearby impasse, the Cité d'Angoulême. The site was the townhouse of the Duke of Angoulême, built in the eighteenth century. All that remains of the grand original is a sculpted pediment; the building, which is surrounded by light industry and housing, was turned over to light industrial use in the early twentieth century and has a plain exterior with large metal-framed windows.

This area of northeastern Paris, stretching from the Place de la Bastille to the Père Lachaise cemetery, is a mixture of three- and four-story apartment houses, small workshops and factories, cafés, shops, and bars. It is hardly a chic area; in fact it is resolutely *populaire*. The novelist Georges Simenon, a writer who understood the ordinary life of Paris better than most, had his detective hero Maigret live on the nearby Boulevard Richard Lenoir. Paris has resisted the transformations of the modern city better than some: there has been neither the flight of the affluent to the suburbs, nor the wholesale expulsion of light industry. Traditional parts of the city have, despite the arrival of fast foods and slow traffic, often kept their character: the Rue du Faubourg St. Antoine, which marks the southern edge of the eleventh arrondisement, is still the center of the furniture industry, as it was in the eighteenth and nineteenth centuries, and the nearby Rue du Temple remains the home of the garment trade, despite two decades of abortive plans to change things. Paris is a small, dense city, architecturally rich and varied, and in choosing to locate his offices in a traditional quarter Nouvel was responding to a desire to stay in touch, in place, and in context.

Within number 10, Cité d'Angoulême, the walls are white or grey, the floors in dark planks. The levels, including a mezzanine inserted over part of the ground floor, are linked by a wide, plain aluminum staircase. On each floor a central open mass of desks and flat files, computer monitors, and architectural models is flanked by individual offices and meeting rooms with glass-topped tables and aluminum chairs. There is bustle and urgency, and the space is a simple backdrop for the work at hand. In the meeting rooms, the walls are deliberately bare. Other architects may hang drawings or photos of recent projects, but at Architectures Jean Nouvel the emphasis is on what *is* happening or *is going* to happen: a meeting with a client is about that client's project, not about past glories. Nouvel himself has no office, preferring to move about, taking a spare chair here, leaning on a desk there, to discuss the development of a project or look at work on a model. Among the fifty employees of the office, a good dozen have been with Nouvel for eight to ten years. Architectures Jean Nouvel is a well-developed team, in which the tastes and abilities of the leading members are well understood among themselves.

The change that created the new company and led to the move to a new location was in part a consequence of the wider changes taking place in French architecture in the early 1990s. President Mitterrand, the creator of so many *grands projets* in the field of architecture, had announced that he would not be standing for a further term. His likely successor, Jacques Chirac, had made it clear that the French treasury would have other preoccupations. The 1980s had seen a series of major state-funded architectural projects. In Paris there had been the Louvre Museum Pyramid and Richelieu wing by I.M. Pei, the Bastille Opera, the new National Library by Dominique Perrault, and the Grande Arche at La Défense to the north of the city itself. Outside Paris one could cite Norman Foster's Médiatheque in Nîmes, Will Alsop's Hôtel du Rhône in Marseille, and Nouvel's own Opera House in Lyon, with countless smaller-scale buildings, such as Geipel and Michelin's CRAFT school in Limoges. The quality of this architectural invest-

Computer-generated image of the Andel building, Prague

ment is without parallel in any other Western country, despite the flurry of new building all over Europe and the United States during the prosperous 1980s.

All the *grands projets* were won in architectural competitions. The French competition system was obligatory for public buildings of almost any size. Whatever its failings, it created opportunities for architects—especially young architects—to make their mark with a large-scale project. The Pompidou Center in Paris justly promoted Richard Rogers and Renzo Piano to the ranks of the master; Nouvel's winning the Institut du Monde Arabe competition gained him international recognition. The relative fairness of the system can also be seen in the opportunities it created for non-French architects, such as Alsop, Pei, and Rogers. For French architects the competition system became a major source of work. (Dominique Perrault once told me that he had never worked for a private customer in twenty or so years of practice—his client had always been the French state.) Nouvel claims, ruefully, to have lost more competitions than any other architect; but then he had more competitions to choose from than most.

By the early 1990s, however, the revenue sources for state commissions were drying up, and projects were increasingly being funded by a mixture of public and private monies. As France faced up to recession and the forthcoming rigors of European monetary union, the country's increasing economic difficulties reduced the opportunities for architects. The competition system itself was falling into discredit if not abeyance. The list of projects awarded but not built got longer, and winning projects were overruled for arbitrary reasons. One striking example of this was Nouvel's own entry for the Grande Stade competition to build a national football stadium in St. Denis, just outside Paris. Contrary to the normal rules, entries were invited from construction companies, not architects, and though Nouvel's project won the jury vote, it was sidelined in favor of a cheaper option which, it is alleged, borrowed a number of features from Nouvel's design. The stadium actually built for France's hosting of the Football World Cup in 1998 attracted criticism before the first ball was kicked: not only had no thought been given to heating the main playing field, but only 5,000 parking spaces had been provided for an estimated 75,000 visitors.

With the change of times, a change of structure was inevitable. Architectures Jean Nouvel is a limited company, not a partnership. The relatively informal ways of working that sufficed for a practice mainly developing projects through competition and dealing with public clients had to give way to a structure that could more effectively face the challenges and opportunities of new markets both in France and overseas. The president and major shareholder of AJN is Michel Pélissié, a long-standing friend of Nouvel's with extensive business experience. Departmental heads for the financial, commercial, and production sectors report to him. Each project has its own budget and *chef de projet*, or job architect, who with a chosen team is responsible for delivering the building. Information technology services, a technical library, and secretarial help provide additional resources. Eric Maria, head of production, sees the system as necessary for the proper functioning of the practice. "All proj-

The Maison Cognacq-Jay

ects are approved by Jean, in consultation with Michel Pélissié, and they choose the team and job architect for each project. Jean is the final arbiter on the design. The job architect is responsible to him for creating the design, and to the management for delivering the project within budget. We are here to monitor and help that process. This sounds cumbersome but works well in practice. The job architects know Nouvel well, understand his values and ways of thinking, and have open access to him, and they rely on us for technical expertise, for example over contractual issues. Jean's role is that of creative director, if you like. He signs each project and building."

With the practice working on sites in France, Switzerland, Austria, and the Czech Republic, and with projects under discussion in Japan, Germany and Italy, some degree of delegation is a necessity. But Nouvel, who works under an exclusive architectural contract for the firm, remains the controlling spirit, responsible for the conception of each design. His design process is as much verbal as visual: each building evolves from an appreciation of its context and from a rational assessment of needs, objectives, and opportunities. His is not simply an architecture of response, nor is it purely ide-

ological, in the sense of applying an existing theoretical framework to every situation. Rather, Nouvel sees each new project as an opportunity to analyze and refine his ideas and principles, to test out theories against the challenge of building. It is from this process of translating ideal to real space, of moving from concept to actual structure, that Nouvel's buildings gain their complexity and energy. This process and the way it operates in his architectural practice are best considered by looking first at a group of current projects and buildings, then turning in later chapters to Nouvel's earlier work, his product and furniture designs, and his views on the purpose, potential, and future of architecture.

Nouvel's built work is of truly international status, and his approach to architecture, based on context, knowledge, and reason, has a great deal to offer to his professional contemporaries. This is because Nouvel's approach is not about dogma or solution, but about logic and method. It is the intellectual quality of his work, as much as its visual appeal, that commands our attention and makes Jean Nouvel one of the most important architects in the world today.

The glass blocks on the exterior of the new construction at Maison Cognacq-Jay have a ridged pattern, designed by Nouvel, that refracts the incident light to create a series of reflections, surface effects, and transparencies depending on the lighting angle.

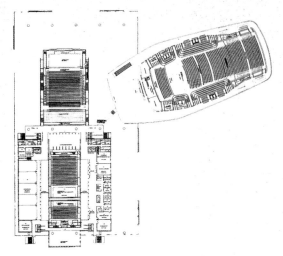

"This is an example of the principle of framing the landscape. It is a building on an exceptional site, by the lake facing the town. The entire town can be seen from the foyer."

Jean Nouvel,
Lecture in Milan, 1995

# Lucerne Kultur und Kongresscentrum

LUCERNE, SWITZERLAND

"I think you will find Lucerne interesting," Nouvel says modestly. Interesting, certainly: it is the first major project to open since the new order—both within his office and in the world of French architecture. So the Lucerne project is both classic Nouvel and new Nouvel, in several senses. First, the gestation time of the project, of which the first phase opened in August 1998 and which will be completed by the year 2000, covers both the current organization, AJN, and its predecessor, JNEC, since the first competition submission was called for in 1989. Second, while there are elements of the design that can be seen as linked to Nouvel's earlier work, there is about the whole conception a new and different approach. Finally, the construction process itself, outside France and under different rules, required the application of both old and new skills.

The original competition invitation for the Lucerne Kultur und Kongresscentrum (KKL) specified creating a new 2,000-seat concert hall alongside the existing smaller Musikhalle building. Nouvel's proposal was to encase the old building in a glass box and project the new hall out over the edge of the lake on which Lucerne is situated, like a new ship caught in mid-launch. This project caught the imagination of the jury and was the winner, but was ruled out in a

ABOVE Nouvel's original design for Lucerne, won in competition in 1989, but rejected in a local referendum

OPPOSITE Color details in the entrance corridor of the main hall

27

referendum, which declared that the line of the lakeshore could not be broken. In fact the two requirements of retaining the old building and respecting the lake meant there was precious little space for the fulfillment of the brief. In 1992 the city of Lucerne invited Nouvel to make a new proposal for a single building, to replace the old one, which would incorporate a main concert hall, a subsidiary hall that could be used for concerts or events, a contemporary art museum, and a conference center, as well as administrative offices and services for all users. The site covers a potential 15,000 square meters.

Lucerne sits at the end of a lake: the two parts of the city face each other across the water and look to the mountains beyond. The surrounding landscape, whether in summer or winter, creates a rich visual backdrop to the historically varied existing architecture and dense urban fabric of the city. A new building had therefore to begin from what Nouvel termed "a principle of inclusion," in which the main element was the lake itself. If the building could not broach the shoreline, the lake would come to the building. Thus the backbone of the building is set away from the lake, and the three principal elements (the two concert halls and the conference center) reach out from this spine towards the lake, divided from each other at ground level by strips of water, a "water garden" in Nouvel's term, crossed by pedestrian bridges. The museum is situated above the western building, the conference center. These elements are unified under an immense sloping copper roof, which projects, unsupported, twenty meters from the main facade, and landmarks the building from the opposite side of the lake.

This layout orients the building to the surrounding city, and at the same time makes visible the functioning of the different elements. The service and administrative areas run along the back spine, with

OPPOSITE Photomontage of the second Lucerne design *in situ*, between the lake and Calatrava's railway station (right)

BELOW (LEFT) Plan for the completed center's ground-floor level, with two inlets from the lake separating the lakefront sections of the building

BELOW (RIGHT) Plan for the completed center's roof, over the main hall (right), smaller hall (center), and museum area (left)

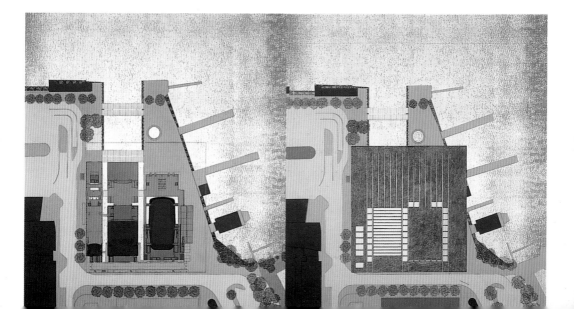

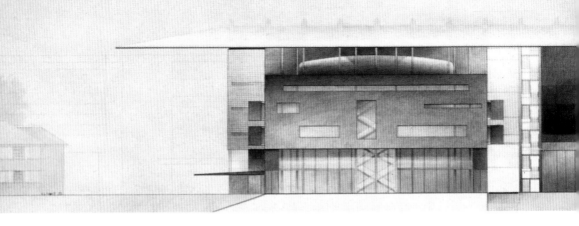

the public areas in front facing the open pedestrian area giving onto the lake. The order of occupation and access thus follows a logical progression. The central unit, the smaller concert hall, has been designed to open completely, if required, onto this public area. From the bar and restaurant area immediately under the roof there is a complete panorama of city and lake, defined and refined by the line of the projecting roof, on which the blue-grey panels of the underside blend into the sky. It becomes a belvedere from which the lake, the city, and their environs can be admired. From the other side of the lake the skyline of the roof marks the position of the building, while the pattern of reflections on the underside of the roof, in daylight but more especially at night, continually maintain the relationship between building and site.

The visual and urban logic of the building flows seamlessly into its organizational aspects, so the service road and service facilities run along the back of the spine, on the opposite side from public access. The Musikhalle was retained and used while the spine and largest concert hall (at the eastern side of the building) were being constructed. Thus the annual music festival, the centerpoint of Lucerne's summer, could take place uninterrupted by the creation of its new home. The new 2,000-seat concert hall opened in August 1998, with the rest of the building due to be finished by December 1999. What Nouvel will have achieved in Lucerne by then is not

LUCERNE KULTUR UND KONGRESSCENTRUM
LUCERNE, SWITZERLAND

only a technical tour de force. He gives each of the elements of the building its own identity within a whole that is both complete in and of itself and integrated into its very special context. In his own words, "the architectural solution has to be harmonious, sensible, intelligent, and inclusive."

The KKL is one of the few buildings under construction in Europe to have its own web site, with live video camera images of the work in progress. Watching concrete set in cyberspace is not just a techno-expression of civic pride: it is the state-of-the-art extension of the complex planning process necessary in Switzerland for the creation of such an important building. The Swiss take local democracy seriously, and projects are submitted to a public referendum before building work begins. In the case of KKL a series of published documents and plans and a program of public meetings and debates were the prelude to not one but four referenda before the final design was adopted. During the building process there have also been regular meetings at which both elected representatives and members of the public have been involved in the progress of the work. The credit for steering the Center through this long and difficult period goes in part to the architect and his team, led by job architect Brigitte Metra, but especially to the former mayor of Lucerne, who initiated the project, and to Thomas Hind, the maître d'oeuvre appointed by the city to deliver the project, who has also

Lakeside elevation of the concert center. For the foyer of the main concert hall (at left), window openings frame specific views. In the smaller hall (center), double-height doors, when open, turn the concert hall into an open-air arena. The grid facade of the museum and conference center (right) continues at side of building

been responsible for supervising the building process for the client. That the project has retained its original purpose, integrity, and conviction throughout is also a tribute to the good sense of the people of Lucerne.

Under the unifying structure of the roof the elements of the building each have their own exterior identity. The service spine is hung on the exterior with a fine green, almost verdigris, metal mesh over the concrete facade, which provides a neutral aspect to the adjoining railway station, designed by Santiago Calatrava. The eastern facade, running along the side of the main concert hall, is marked by deep blue boxes on the exterior of the access passages, with burgundy red for the intervening spaces. Along the western side, covering the museum and conference center, a silver-grey rectangular metal grid will be hung. This grid will turn the corner onto the main facade, covering the front of the congress center and museum. The rest of the main lakefront facade is divided by the waterways. For the main concert hall, there is a deep glazed foyer rising from ground level through the first three floors. Layers of glass set to the plane of the facade and at right angles to it provide a literal and metaphorical reflection of the clear waters of the lake. The next three levels, up to the terrace immediately under the roof, are also faced in deep blue, with a series of picture windows of different sizes. These windows are set on predetermined sightlines, framing the major monuments of the city and key features of the surrounding landscape such as the mountains. Thus the theme of inclusion, of exterior flowing into interior, is maintained even within the closed space of the upper foyer. The middle element of the facade, fronting the smaller concert hall and part of the museum, is a monolithic dark grey sheet of polished concrete over a glazed entrance. The same dark surface is used for the side walls of the building units where they divide over the channels of water from the lake to rejoin the spine.

The differentiated handling of the exterior facades is not necessary merely to give texture and value to what might, in another architect's hands, have been a rigid and uncomfortable mass set in the urban and natural landscape. It also is an external expression of the internal design. The external grid for the museum area (which sits under the roof over the conference center) echoes the rigid division of the museum's internal spaces into equal cubes, a scheme devised by the artist Remy Zaugg in keeping with the collection of often minimalist contemporary work that forms the core of the museum's holdings. The cubes will be finished in white, lit from overhead through daylight diffusers in the ceilings. At one point, a large window will break the pattern of regularity to offer an exterior view, framing the Pilatus mountain behind the city. The central 900-seat hall will be a dark and magical space, appropriate both for the sumptuous feasts of a civic banquet or the popular bustle of a pop or folk concert, when the full-height doors into the foyer and from the foyer onto the promenade can be opened to accommodate a larger audience. This sequence of facades and interiors developed in response to the initial brief and the demands of the design as it evolved.

ABOVE View of Lucerne from the roof terrace of the KKL

OVERLEAF (LEFT) Interior of the main concert hall, showing the plain white finish; (RIGHT) The concert hall as it will appear during a performance, with the acoustic doors open

The brief for the main concert hall, which was to seat just under 2,000, was simple: the best concert hall in the world. Nouvel worked with the American acoustic engineer Russell Johnson and his team at Artec in New York on the acoustic specifications. The main hall has four rows of balconies above the raked stalls floor; completely flexible stage machinery; and a hanging acoustic reflector that can change level to suit the performance. Artec suggested modifying the initial internal volumes for a better effect (the first proposal was too long in relation to its height and width), and including two additional features. The first of these is an "echo chamber" built around the upper part of the hall, nine meters deep. Two rows of doors around the top two balconies, each two meters wide, open onto this space. The concrete doors, faced with plaster, are on motor-driven hinges, and a computerized control system allows each door to be positioned exactly between fully closed and open to 90 degrees outwards into the echo chamber, thereby subtly modifying the acoustical effect according to the wishes of the conductor or the demands of the music being performed. Secondly, the acousticians suggested patterning the door and wall surfaces with a series of indentations to increase the depth of the acoustic effect. The final design for these patterns, punched into the plaster surfaces at close intervals, was decided by Nouvel and Artec together.

The variable door concept is a specialty of Russell Johnson's, and music lovers and acoustic specialists will no doubt continue to debate its contribution to the nuances of the hall. But the aesthetic treatment of doors and the plaster patterns was integral to Nouvel's final visual solution. In the first model, though the doors are incorporated, the interior is shown with plain wall surfaces painted in decreasing tones of red and blue with a black ceiling. When Nouvel saw the finished, unpainted interior he decided to keep it white, since the patterning of the plaster created a sufficiently strong effect. The interior walls of the echo chamber, however, would be painted red and crosslit from within by track-

The foyer of the main concert hall and the shell of the auditorium

1|20

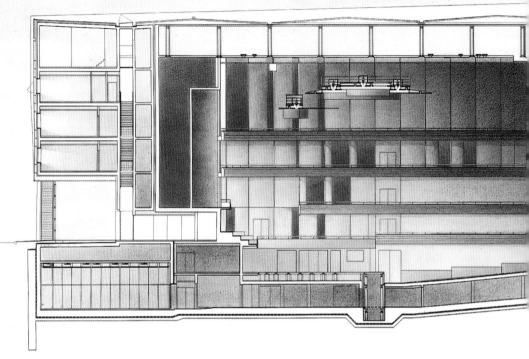

mounted spotlights. Depending on the door apertures, the audience would see different patterns and intensities of red edging the upper parts of the hall, an effect accentuated by painting red cloud patterns on the otherwise black ceiling. For these special lighting effects and the general interior lighting, Nouvel called on the internationally famous lighting designer Ingo Maurer, while the paint effects were created by Alain Bonny, who works regularly with Nouvel and who also advised on the external color scheme.

The new interior design, with its strong monochrome patterning streaked by lines of red from the doors and muted by the blue seating, is a jewel: calm but rigorous, welcoming, and relaxed. The different sizes of patterning on the facades of the balconies and on the walls and doors—the former more a line of shapes than the dense granularity of the latter—recall the varied urban and natural den-

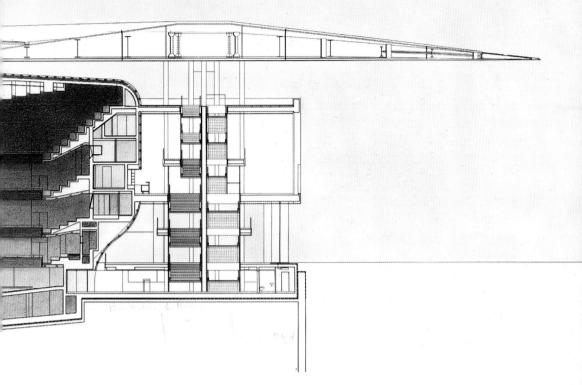

sities of the surrounding city and country. The same *urbs in rure, rus in urbe* balance can be found in the broad vista from the terrace below the roof, where the spectator's gaze moves across the city itself and is drawn by the broadening expanse of the lake towards the distant pastures, crowned by the mountains of the Alps. Here the effect of the projecting roof comes into its own, framing the field of view, with its outermost point an astonishing 45 meters on the diagonal from the building itself. What Nouvel has achieved at Lucerne is a masterpiece of synthesis and expression, responding to the needs of a visually dense site yet creating a wholly contemporary building whose function is clearly readable through its bold subtleties.

Original design color sketch for the interior of the main concert hall. After the main plasterwork was completed and the acoustic doors installed, Nouvel was pleased with the effect and decided not to implement the colors in this sketch.

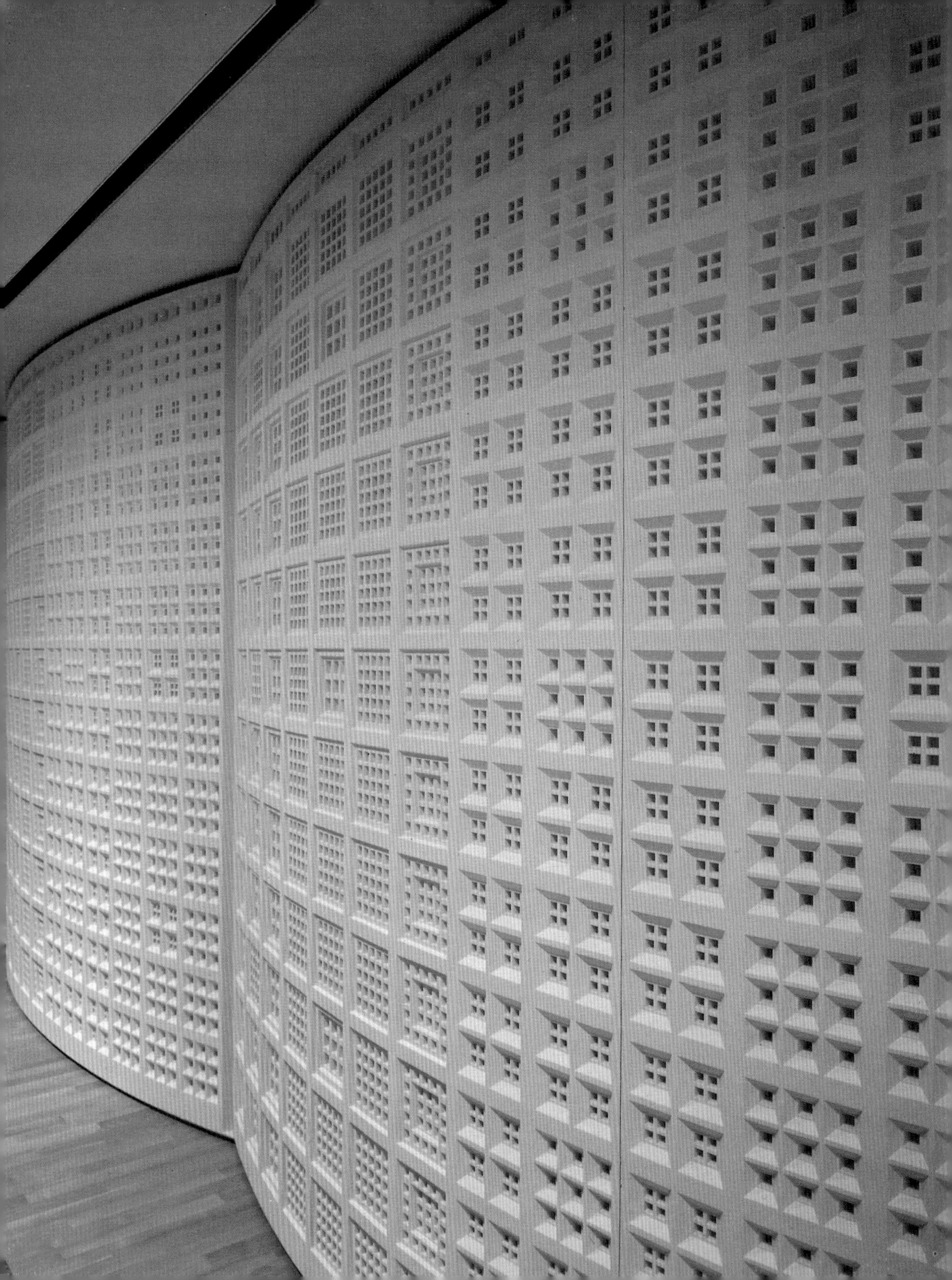

ABOVE The entrance corridor to
the main auditorium, with color
effects by Alain Bonny

OPPOSITE The patterned plasterwork on the acoustic doors in the
main auditorium

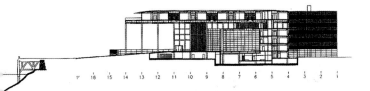

# Cité Justiciaire

NANTES, FRANCE

"I am just trying to find the just definition of an architecture of justice," Jean Nouvel punned in his 1993 competition submission for the Cité Justiciaire, or courtroom complex, at Nantes in the Loire Valley in central France. This approach to the brief, while it may seem simple, underlines a profound and complex issue, for as he points out, the architecture of officialdom is the representation of power. Thus, a courthouse makes a statement about the power of the state, its law, order, and justice. Historically, public buildings carried a high semantic content of power; this continued to be so in the twentieth century, in the work of Albert Speer in Berlin and Leonid Semenov in Moscow, for example. This is a significant symbolic tradition. At Nantes Nouvel has overlaid these traditional signs of power with a contemporary conception of justice in a wholly modern building.

The site for the new court building is a disused naval dockyard on the edge of the Loire River, across from the main center of Nantes. The structure must make an impact from a distance, without necessarily obstructing the skyline. Nouvel's approach was to set the building at the top of a broad, shallow ramp leading up from the river; the main entrance would thus face the water. Behind the river-

ABOVE Section drawing

OPPOSITE Computer-generated drawing of the main hall. The large size of this building was in part dictated by its function; it houses both a courthouse and complete legal services.

43

side facade is the principal public area, giving access to the courtrooms behind this (on the ground floor and above), with the court
and police offices and prison area at the back of the building overlooking a park. Avenues of trees leading to the park frame the sides
of the complex, and between the main units of the internal structure
there are clear views to the park. In plan, the building is square, a
deliberate statement of even regularity which carries through the
structure as its functional and unifying motif.

The whole complex is based on scaling up and down from an 8-
meter x 8-meter grid. This is not simplicity for simplicity's sake, or
even *rigor de rigueur*. It is a direct visual metaphor for the concepts
of fairness and equity, balance and justice that underpin the practice of law. The grid represents a transference between the
definition of justice and the constructed sign. This application of
order does not merely apply in plan (where the floor tiles, in polished
grey granite, are in units of 64 one-meter-square tiles or 256 25-
centimeter tiles, and the ceiling coffers are in units of four, sixteen,
or sixty-four) but also to the elevation. The 110-meter building is
13.75 meters high—one-eighth as high as it is broad or long.

This formal approach could become oppressive, its regularity dead-
ening. But the metaphor is about the fairness and openness of justice, not its formalities. The application of the principle is therefore
given complexity by variety in scale, by detailing, and by light. For
variety in scale, let us look at two instances. The function of the
building moves from open to closed, from public to private, in
receding planes from front to back. The grid is at its most open on
the public side, 8 meters wide by 12 meters high, while the metal
grill that closes the back of the building to the park, at a distance
of 4 meters (for fire access) from the rear wall, is on a 12.5-
centimeter mesh. As the building runs north–south, this means the
southern, closed, edge gets the best protection from sunlight and
glare. Within the main waiting hall, there are full-depth glass
screens, both to create independent areas and to reduce noise levels, parallel to the main facade. Between these, rows of columns
support the roof. The span between the columns (which are of 50-
centimeter-square sections) is 15 meters, edge to edge. Not only is
this a considerable feat of technology, it also creates a sense of
soaring space that transcends the regularities of the basic system
without breaking its rules.

Drawing of the main facade of the
complex, showing the direct sightlines through the building to the
park and the grid system for
columns, doors, and windows

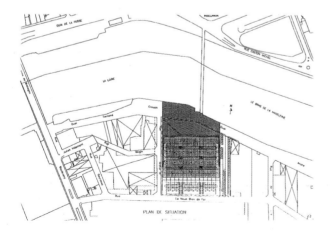

PLAN DE SITUATION

As to detailing, it is a matter of principle for Nouvel that basic structural elements be concealed (unlike some architects for whom exposed eyebolts and visible nuts are the very expression of authentic creativity). At Nantes he insisted on minimum interference with the linear expression of the grid elements. Glass meets metal without glazing bars or lips.

Light is the third element that humanizes the grid. First, the exterior walls are largely glazed, allowing for continuous interaction between the formality of the constructed interior and the natural variety of river parkland and sky on the exterior. Second, the gaps between the internal units of the building and the surrounding largely public space bring daylight into the interior as well as opening perspectives onto the park and river. Third, there is the deliberate use of natural light in the courtrooms themselves. While these are closed on the outside, each courtroom is lit from above by a lightwell that is aligned to one of the "light channels" in the roof itself. This lightwell is in turn positioned so that the bulk of the light from it falls on the bench where the judges, magistrates, or assessors sit. This piece of natural theater embodies a central principle of justice: that it be open and clear, operating in public and in the light.

At the ground-floor level, as we have noted, there are three units within the building that contain the principal courtrooms (with the Assize Court in the center), with a further suite of courts—the Tribunal de Grande Instance—at an upper level. Immediately below the roof there is a floor of private offices for the judges and for senior court officials. The offices at the front open on to a roof ter-

OPPOSITE (ABOVE) Design drawing for one of the courtrooms. The ceiling lightwell directs natural light onto the judges' bench, while the interior design repeats and maintains the grid of the exterior.

OPPOSITE (BELOW) Site plan

ABOVE Computer rendering of the court building in relation to the river and the city and the proposed pedestrian bridge across the river

OVERLEAF Computer-generated drawing of the north elevation of the complex. Its sloping esplanade to the Loire River affords a view into the heart of the city on the other bank.

CITÉ JUSTICIAIRE
NANTES, FRANCE

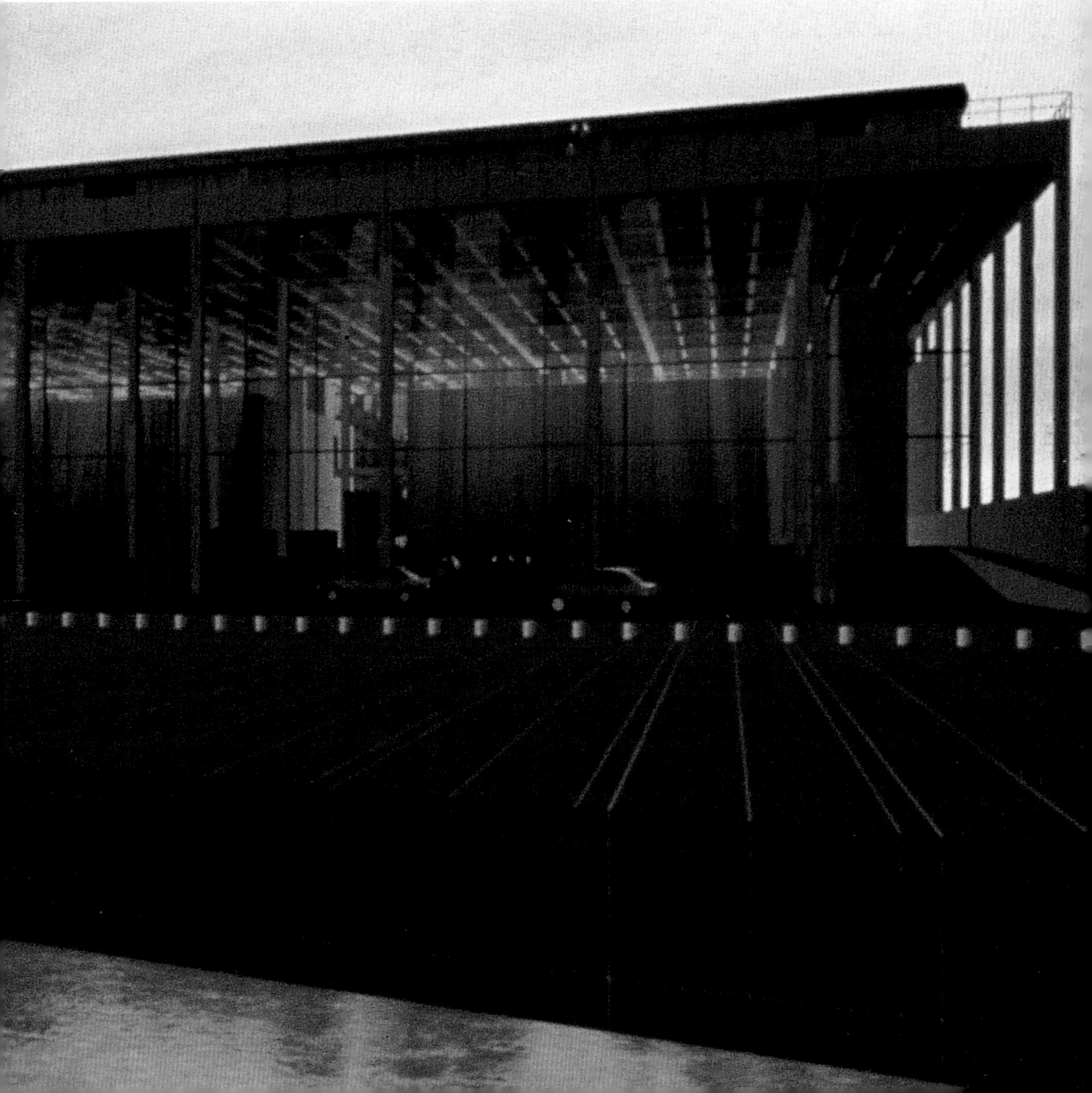

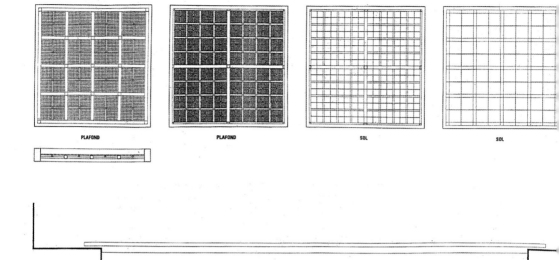

PLAFOND          PLAFOND          SOL          SOL

race overlooking the river, and those behind onto the "light channels" that admit daylight to the courtrooms. The light channels form the central part of the floor of the passageways between the offices. The passages are covered on each side, but otherwise open to the sky. This touch brings light through the whole building, not just its main volume.

When the Cité Justiciaire opens in the autumn of 1999 it will not only provide a service, it will offer a model of justice for the twenty-first century—justice not as the power of the state bearing down on the individual, but as a process of regularity and equality, operating in a formal and ordered context. Nouvel describes the Nantes building as moving "from the definition of justice to its representation in architecture." This he has achieved without the traditional symbolism of swords, scales, and blindfolds, in a building whose integrity and elegance state its purpose with intelligence and clarity.

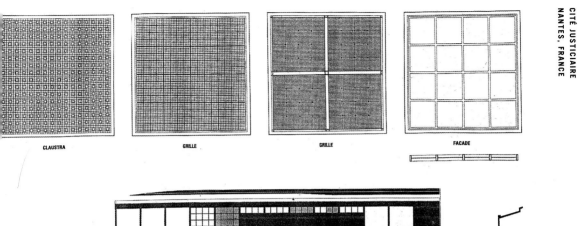

CLAUSTRA     GRILLE     GRILLE     FACADE

ABOVE Varying densities of grid and different arrangements of elements within the eight-meter square, as presented in the competition submission

BELOW Preliminary section showing the relationship of grid elements to the progression of the building, front to back, and the proposed footbridge over the Loire River

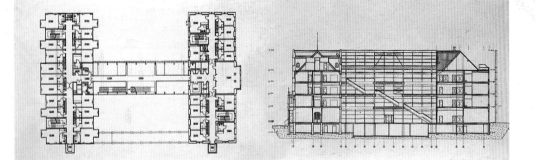

# Maison Cognacq-Jay

RUEIL, FRANCE

The Cognacq-Jay family founded the Samaritaine department store in Paris in the late nineteenth century. The family shared their prosperity with their fellow citizens, endowing a museum in Paris and donating their art collection to it. As good employers they provided a day-care center for their employees' children and a health insurance plan. In time they also found they needed a retirement home for their employees, and bought a former girls' school situated in a park on the outskirts of Paris for this purpose. The original building had been designed as "a French version of an English version of neo-Gothic": it is a flat-fronted building with a sharply pitched roof. It is now run by a mutual health insurance group, though it still carries the Cognacq-Jay name. In 1995 the owners decided to renovate and extend the property, and invited Jean Nouvel to undertake the work.

The plan of the original building was based on axial corridors on each floor—far from a modern arrangement. But the option of razing the old building and starting afresh was not possible on either financial or logistical grounds. The brief instead called for doubling the available accommodation, and adding new office premises and day-care facilities. As the position of the existing building on the tri-

ABOVE The ground-floor plan shows how the new building mirrors the old. The central administrative unit forms the bar of the H between the two.

OPPOSITE View of the administration building that forms the crossbar of the new structure

ABOVE The original girls' school,
with the new building behind it

OPPOSITE View from inside
the original building to the new
construction, with the administrative unit between

angular site had a determining logic of its own, Nouvel decided to
respect this, and make his addition symmetrical to the original. Taking the existing building as the downstroke of a capital letter H, he
added a new "crossbar" building, intended for the office and other
facilities, and a parallel downstroke for the accommodation. The
symmetry that began in plan extended to other elements of the
design. The roof and floor heights, and the roof angles for both the
crossbar and the mirror building were also based on the original
structure, as were the corridor arrangements. The fenestration plan
is also a mirror image of the existing building.

The arrangement of the building is quite conventional: the solution
of matching blocks joined by a central crossbar is wholly logical.
What is astonishing is the exterior treatment of the new structure.
Rather than imitating the cornices and stucco work of the old building, Nouvel decided to coat the whole structure in glass, not so as
to make a transparent building—an inappropriate solution for a
residential building—but rather a glazed one. The exterior walls
and roof are finished in plain rendered concrete. Over this surface

a series of metal frames, based on a 40-by-40-centimeter grid, is suspended, each framing a profiled molded glass block. The molding on the surface of the blocks, of half-rhomboids arranged in a diagonal pattern, was designed by Nouvel. The same treatment is used on the roof. The result is part mirror, part jewel, ambiguous in its transparent solidity.

This idea of doubling a building with its mirror image has been used before by Nouvel, for a summer school at Kerjuanno in Brittany in 1981, during what the author Patrice Goulet aptly terms Nouvel's "guerrilla" period. At Kerjuanno the weight of local planning regulations almost forbade an intelligent solution, so Nouvel played the rules against themselves. The two facades match on the blueprint plan. But in the finished building one is black, the other white; one has large windows in narrow frames, the other has narrow windows framing a blank recess, and so on. The Cognacq-Jay building is both more mature and subtler; not a manifesto but a manifestation of an architectural intention to devise an original and coherent solution to the challenge of brief and site.

This solution creates what might be termed an abstract double of the original (the second phase of the project will be to recondition the earlier building): a double in that the proportions and layout of the original are mirrored in the new, and abstract in the sense of the new construction's invisibility. This design solution is a stage in a process, for which dematerialization is a description but not a definition, that begins with the Tour Sans Fins, continues through the MediaPark project and achieves another, different expression in the Cartier building. At the heart of this evolution is the assumption that the materiality of architecture does not have to be evident in the final building.

The rear of the new building, showing the glass blocks on the facades and the "bow windows" for the residents' rooms

# Euralille Development

LILLE, FRANCE

If one were looking for a single project that could sum up some of
the changes that have taken place in recent years in French architecture, the redevelopment of part of Lille, in northeastern France,
would be a good candidate. First, the need for change was driven by
external forces: in this case the building of the Channel Tunnel and
the start of a direct rail service from Paris to London, and the
extension of the French high-speed train system into northeastern
France and Belgium. Second, the project was a joint venture
between state and private capital. Third, the architects were
appointed after an invitation to an interview, not through a competition. And fourth, different parts of the total program were under-
taken by different architects, under the general direction of Rem
Koolhaas and his Office for Metropolitan Architecture. He invited
Nouvel to create for Euralille a complex of shops and offices at the
center of the new program.

Lille, through its mayor, Pierre Mauroy, realized that the transport
initiative could revitalize a city where traditional industry, as in so
much of northern Europe, had been under pressure. The new transport links would put 50 million people (equivalent to almost the
whole population of France or of England) within ninety minutes'

Accommodation units at Euralille.
Note the use of colored panels
and screenprinted colors on the
glazing.

OVERLEAF The interior of the
commercial center at Euralille. The
slope of the roof follows the contours of the site, which links the
main rail station with the new
high-speed train station.

travel of the city. The opportunity to create a service and consumer
industry hub for this region was obvious. The way to achieve this,
ironically, was to clear old fortifications, built to keep Belgians and
Germans at bay, and use the site for the new rail station, hotel,
office, and shopping facilities. To do this also meant moving underground the highway that had previously cut the center of Lille off
from its periphery, and building the largest underground car park
in Europe.

Koolhaas felt it was important for the overall scheme to make the
new station as visible as possible. Nouvel's site is roughly triangular in plan, with the southwest corner next to the existing SNCF
railway station, and the opposite northern side flanking the new
high-speed train station. The building slopes down towards the TGV
station, partly following the slope of the land. The brief was to de-

liver two floors of shops together with a series of five additional units: two for the Lille business school, two as sports center, and one as a cultural center, all under a single roof, together with access to five towers (of which three have been constructed to date, one as offices, one as a hotel, and one as student lodgings for the business school). These towers line the southern facade of the building; on the western side there is another hotel, a housing block, and offices and accommodation for SNCF personnel.

The floor plan for the commercial center at Euralille is best understood through its function of linking the two railway stations, of bridging the gap between center and periphery formerly created by the highway. The main entrance is onto the SNCF station. This corridor crosses, at an angle, another main artery halfway through the building, which opens on the north facade opposite the high-speed train station. This deliberate irregularity not only creates interesting shop plans but also a range of different and unexpected perspectives, especially on the upper floors, under the slope of the roof.

The roof itself is just over four hectares in area, comprising an openwork metal grid set on top of an asphalt surface. Colored lights and patterns on this surface, like the coded abstract signage of airport runways, create strange and dimly perceived patterns from above the grid. As one of the job architects, Isabelle Guillauic, points out, "It is one of the most exciting spaces I have ever worked on, and I'm one of the lucky few who have been able to be inside it." Lighting an unoccupied roof space is not mere whim or decoration. The roof plays an important role in linking the disparate elements of the large site. In addition, for Nouvel, light, materials, and color are as important as form and volume in the definition of architectural space.

This principle has been carried over onto the facades of the shopping center and towers. Over a neutral grey background a series of immense holographic images has been silkscreened. They create patterns that echo and accompany the signage of individual shops, establishing the immateriality of the architecture on its very surface.

BELOW Screenprinted images on the external glazing—a classic method Nouvel uses to integrate his buildings with their sites

OPPOSITE Two details of the silkscreening on the exterior at Euralille

# Schmikov Quarter

PRAGUE, CZECH REPUBLIC

The fall of the Iron Curtain and the end of Soviet domination in Eastern Europe has created problems and opportunities in fairly equal measure. In architecture and urbanism, cities and communities have had to evolve new ways of thinking about and organizing development to replace Soviet centralized planning. Nouvel found the opportunities in Prague, where he advised on the urban planning for the Schmikov area of the city. He was then commissioned by a private client who had sponsored the initial study, part of the Dutch-Swiss ING banking and investment group, to build two projects, due for delivery by the end of this century.

The Schmikov quarter, about 500 acres, is located across the Ultava river from the historic center of Prague. Mainly built in the nineteenth century as a mix of worker housing and light industry, it was run-down and in places derelict. The last proposal from the old regime was to build an urban motorway through Schmikov. For Nouvel, the study became an exercise in methodology rather than a planning proposal. The urban motorway should go away, or, if it was essential, go underground: any surface route would simply disrupt the area further, breaking it into isolated segments. The team looked at the area street by street and created a map of local activity as a

ABOVE Aerial view of the Schmikov Quarter showing Nouvel's system of spot intervention in color

OPPOSITE Details of three projects at Schmikov: signage gantries rising like marker flags above the roofline of a shopping center (top); the old brewery building, relit and linked to the adjoining building by an electronic facade (center); and the "hedgehog" building, refurbished and relit (bottom)

basis for action. Nouvel proposed to redevelop key sites as areas for public access, based on the theory that increased activity in each segment would create new lines of communication and so generate renewal and redevelopment from within. Imposing solutions from outside might either fail or drive the existing population out of the area. His approach was that of a watercolor painter putting dots of pigment onto a damp sheet of paper: gradually the color stains outwards, until the whole sheet is tinted. This was a pointillist approach, which depended for its success on an understanding of the current dynamics of the area; each intervention was made to gain maximum effect. For example, the "hedgehog" building has long been empty and disused, and is covered in scaffolding to keep it from collapsing. Nouvel proposed to paint it in yellow, gold, and white and light it at night; what had been an eyesore, a blot on the landscape, would become a focal point. When the interior was eventually renovated—as a café, or cinema, or whatever—the scaffolding and lighting would remain as a feature. This is a slow process, but by respecting existing uses and activity, the disruption and dispersal of the local population that a large-scale rebuilding would inevitably cause is avoided. A slow process would also follow the learning curve of the new, independent Czech Republic.

The ING's investment program in Prague is directed by Paul Koch, who is, according to Frédérique Monjanel, job architect for the two building projects, "that rare client who has an absolute policy of quality." (Koch was also responsible for inviting Frank Gehry to build in Prague.) For the ING's own offices he had selected a riverside site, next to the quays for the pleasure boats that make trips on the Ultava in the summer. The project is dominated by a 40-meter tower that sits in the water, framed by an L-shaped office block, six stories high. Local planning regulations required that roof heights, zoning, and roof angles conform to the surrounding buildings, so both tower and office building have saddleback roofs.

The tower roof has a very exaggerated slope, modeled on the warning towers that had been built on the river to prevent flooding. These towers were erected over wells, into which the water of the river could be diverted when it rose too high; the towers also provided

OPPOSITE Two computer-generated views of the new ING headquarters building on the riverfront of the Schmikov Quarter. Between the buildings and the river are a large open summer cafe and embarkation points for river steamers.

vantage points. Both the new tower and office block are finished in monochrome copper, which will patinate naturally with time. Since the seasonal changes of climate in Prague are severe, the eastern and northern facades have been well insulated, with fewer openings and good artificial light, while the more sheltered southern and western facades are more open.

The Andel building in the Schmikov Quarter of Prague is Nouvel's most ambitious project there. The finished building will contain 13,000 square meters of office space and 7,000 square meters of shops, with the possibility of converting part of the offices into housing at a later date. The site sits over a subway station that handles 20,000 passengers each day. The project has been planned as four linked buildings, joined by walkways, with a large communal roof garden on top. The southern, eastern, and western facades face onto streets, the north onto a housing complex. The long southern facade is slightly curved to follow the line of the street. At the southeastern corner the building rises into a curved half-drum shape.

It is the treatment of the street facades that mark this project. Over the white and grey concrete framing and the glazed windows of the upper stories, a series of texts and images will be silkscreened in monochrome: a poem by Jan Palach; a view of clouds; a gigantic image of an angel on the half-drum end building. This has the practical value of reducing solar gain in the summertime, and both marking the building and integrating it into its urban context. At street level, above the shops, a double row of projecting angled canopies will carry a stream of publicity, creating animation and marking off the two purposes of the building.

OPPOSITE Computer-generated image of the Andel building, showing the angel motif on the main tower

"When I paint smoke, it should be so
that you can hammer a nail into it."

Pablo Picasso

# Concert Hall

LUXEMBOURG

If the Fondation Cartier building represents one solution to the
problem of the immaterial building designed as a series of planes,
the Luxembourg Concert Hall attempts a resolution of an immaterial, fully three-dimensional space—an evident paradox. Why
attempt this here? The answers lie partly in the site and partly in
the building's purpose. The site is part of a new development—the
"European quarter" overlooking the old city of Luxembourg on one
side and parkland on the other. Thus the building is a belvedere, and
the essential quality of a belvedere is that you see it as little as possible in order to see more. The building's function, of course, is to
showcase music. In his competition submission, Nouvel articulated
the contradictory roles of these two arts: "In the year 2000, if
architecture is the setting into stone of living sensations and emotions, it must carry the inscription of our time, based here on
researching the correspondence between the immaterial nature of
music and the inexorable materiality of architecture."

Nouvel proposed what he called a *mono-matière-mutable*, a unified
but changeable material. "Imagine a building," he suggests, "which
is four-fifths opaque and with the last fifth changing progressively
from opacity to complete transparency. As you moved around it and

OPPOSITE View of the model for
the Luxembourg Concert Hall,
showing the use of *mono-matière-
mutable*

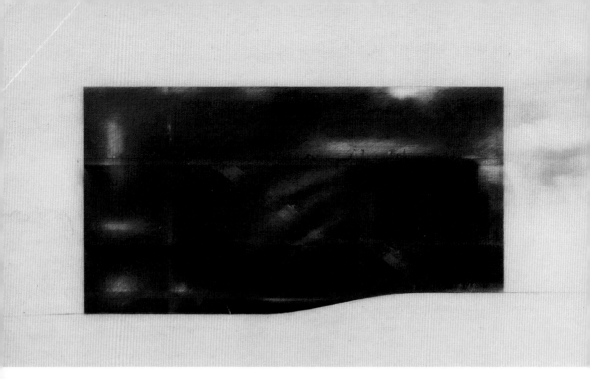

within it, its appearance would change. From the exterior, a corner seemingly solid from one viewpoint would disappear as the viewpoint changed. The whole concept of a wall being intersected, in an interior, by another wall, would be changed by making the intersection invisible. It's the creation of a precise fog—now that's an expression I've always liked."

This precise fog is achieved by using a uniform pale grey color for opaque material and the same color screenprinted onto glass in different densities from opacity to transparency. At certain angles the exterior form of the building is clear, but the placement and extent of openings or forms within the building is not. This is not merely a redefinition of immateriality in architecture. It is a resolute attempt to define a new sense of architectural space, one based on temporal, rather than linear, measurement. Nouvel's work has repeatedly addressed this problem—in the conception of interior spaces, as at the Institut du Monde Arabe, as a sequence of film shots from a storyboard; by the progressive compression of interior densities as one moves through the interior of the Cité Justiciaire; in the physical evanescence of the proposed design for Tour Sans Fins; the

ABOVE Rendering of the Concert Hall's exterior

OPPOSITE Interior section for the main auditorium

combined interiority and exteriority of the cones at the Galeries Lafayette; and the planar games with shadows and reflections in the Fondation Cartier. The Luxembourg Concert Hall, had it been built, would have shown a further development of this theme, which resumes many of Nouvel's central concerns with the relationship between the contemporary building and its urban context.

In his book *Esthétique de la Disparution,* Paul Virilio makes the point that technology, particularly the technology of high-speed transport, has changed our understanding of time in an unprecedented way, moving it from the concept of a fixed present to that of a perspective, in which the mutability of movement itself (through acceleration and change of speed) is a further destabilizing factor, creating the further paradox that "it is extreme movement which creates the inertia of the instant. The instantaneous will create the instant of time! So that in the end the instant will be like the illusory perception of stability, clearly revealed by the technology we use."

Nouvel's determination to use contemporary technology, and the concepts of the computer, cinema, and virtuality as tools for the expression of a continuously relevant modernity, expressed though architecture, are all embedded in the complexities of the Luxembourg project. It is a philosophical but practical statement about the function of architecture today.

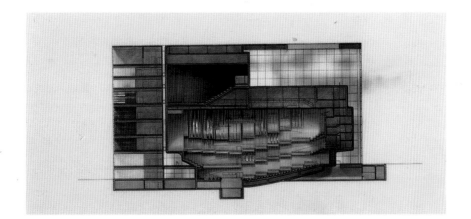

OPPOSITE Close-up of the model, revealing the scale and the transparency effects

ABOVE This view of the model shows the varying degrees of opacity and transparency.

OPPOSITE Nouvel's exhibition design for the Paris Biennale. This continuing contact with contemporary art through the 1980s was important for his current and future work.

LEFT Classroom in the Collège Anne Franck, Antony, France

# In the Beginning

Jean Nouvel was born in Fumel, near Cahors in southwestern France, in 1945. His parents (his father was a school inspector, his mother a language teacher) moved when he was eight years old to the medieval town of Sarlat, also in the Lot et Garonne region. The area, well known for its wines, is mainly small farming country, reasonably prosperous, with Bordeaux to the northwest as its main urban center, rather than Paris, further northeast, or Toulouse to the southeast. "My parents were quite strict with me," he once recalled. "No comic books, no going to the cinema. So I hid the comic books under my bed, and climbed over the garden wall to go to the cinema, arranging to get in after the start and leave before the end—fiendishly complicated. I acquired a taste for forbidden things young!"

Preschool at Trelissac, Dordogne, France

He wanted to be a painter, but again his parents said no. Architecture, then? Yes, provisionally: first in Bordeaux, then at the Ecole de Beaux-Arts in Paris. Nouvel won first place in the school's entrance competition, and in 1966 went to Paris. "A friend met me at the station, and we took the métro. We walked all the way along the platform so as to not to waste time when we changed trains later—an incomprehensible idea for someone from the country!" At first Nouvel thought of trying to change back to painting after a year in architecture, but within a year he had taken a job with architect Claude Parent, who promptly put him in charge of a site under construction. (Nouvel was later to use this "learn to swim at the deep end" approach with new staff of his own.) If Parent's office was a practical one, it was also a hotbed of theory. "I used to discuss catastrophe theory with Paul Virilio only in the afternoons, when Parent wasn't about," Nouvel once recalled, "as Parent accused him of reducing productivity."

Paris in the late 1960s was also politically turbulent, erupting in May 1968. Every official institution in France came under question, including the Ecole. Nouvel took the floor at the amphitheater in the Sorbonne to protest the academicism of the Beaux-Arts system and the conservatism and self-interest of the Ordre des Architectes, the official body for architects. He also argued the stupidities of centralized planning and the failures of postwar urban reconstruction. (When it came to finally qualifying from the Beaux-Arts, instead of the set of finished drawings normally required, Nouvel submitted a text—which was refused.)

The open debates and street democracy of 1968 enabled Nouvel to clarify his own perception of the legitimacy of the architectural act. As he said in a recent interview, "I arrived at that time at a clear distinction between the democratic and the cultural aspects of architecture, and it was immediately evident that each had their own autonomy. You can decide democratically issues of location, program, use, but the aesthetic act is not negotiable. Ultimately the task of architecture is precisely to create the cultural definition of the built environment." This duality of obligation, the architect's responsibility to a public and to his or her own personal integrity, is a crucial aspect of Nouvel's approach to architecture.

In 1970 he left Parent's office to set up his own practice with a colleague, François Seigneur, and Parent generously gave him several projects to get started. This phase of Nouvel's career has been aptly termed by Patrice Goulet "the guerrilla period": lost competitions, battles with planners over absurd regulations, discussion and argument, lectures and publications. Not at all unusual for a young practice, this period established patterns of thought, intervention, and reflection that were to bear fruit later.

In 1974, François Seigneur moved on, and Nouvel built a new team, in which the theater director Jacques Marquet played a major role as a consultant. The late 1970s showed a crop of real projects: a clinic at Bezons, a school at Antony, and a theater at Belfort. In 1980 the practice moved to the rue Lacuée near the Bastille, and won the Institut du Monde Arabe project. Nouvel created the design together with Lézénès and Soria and Architecture Studio. This was a collaboration of too much talent, and the architects were ultimately unable to work together.

Delbigot House

In February 1984 the French magazine *L'Architecture d'aujourd'hui* published what was in effect a special issue on Jean Nouvel. In a frank personal statement, he set out his approach to architecture. "An architect," Nouvel points out,

> cannot know in advance every element that has to be integrated into a final project. There are questions to be put, answers to be understood. . . . The aim of this is to acquire all the available data. So I find myself in favor of a dialogue starting between those who have a right to make demands about the project, for political or social reasons, for example, or those who are going to use or live in the building, and those whose experience gives them information. I am for this dialogue being participatory because in terms of the uses of the building, I am for integrating every properly founded demand. I would go further: I would give the responsibility for the location of functions and equipment . . . to those actively engaged in the project. The role of the architect is the technical and cultural definition of the building, and for transforming ideas into reality. In short, let's define responsibilities, each to his own. But that doesn't mean I am looking for some impossible cultural consensus—that's a route to grey mediocrity. Not an architecture for the greatest number, rather an architecture of individuality, seeing architecture as a specific response. The only constant is that every architectural act, in each place, at each time, must be the act that is the right one.

This insistence on the specificity of the project is matched by an equal insistence on the breadth of cultural openness and knowledge an architect

Summer school building at Kerjuano, Brittany, France

Staircase at the Delvodère House

must bring to a project. "If this is contradictory, so be it! A knowledge of history implies using what is known to understand what is unknown and in turn explore that. It encourages one to identify errors, to flush out those areas which one thought were understood but were not. You can call this approach a philosophical one: I think of it in Michel Foucault's terms, as 'an archaeology of knowledge.' It represents an interest in or a taste for historical moments of rupture, emergence, and change. The essential things to be said or proved are to be found precisely in such zones of discontinuity." Nouvel's work, especially after the Institut du Monde Arabe, was going to show the importance of identifying, understanding, and resolving the inherent contradictions in contemporary architecture and society. It is not an architectural program, in the sense of a set of rules to be applied; rather it is a profound and subtle approach to architecture, both as a philosophy and a practice.

In 1984 Nouvel set up a new partnership in parallel to his own practice with some of his job architects. This period saw the INIST building in Nancy (page 188), the Nemausus housing development in Nîmes (104), the Lyon Opera House (page 118), the Tour Sans Fins (page 154), and the Onyx Cultural Center at St. Herblain (page 182), as well as a whole gamut of competition projects, many lost, some won but never built, each an opportunity to explore a possibility, to evolve a form of architectural response. The staff level rose to over seventy, and Nouvel realized he needed a business manager. In 1988 he invited Emmanuel Cattani to become his partner.

Cattani, a graduate of Lausanne Polytechnic, was an established technical architect who brought with him a number of industrial and political connections—the St. Poulain factory at Blois was a project he initiated. But the change did little to reduce the pressure at the top, and Ibos and Vitart left. Then recession set in, leading to a further restructuring, and the creation of Architectures Jean Nouvel.

One constant element in Nouvel's working method through all these changes is the involvement of outsiders, particularly from the arts, in the project team. Claude Parent introduced Nouvel to the world of contemporary art, and the role of Jacques Le Marquet has already been mentioned. Nouvel once said of Le Marquet, "he taught me to read the truths of fiction." For over a decade Nouvel was architectural advisor to the Paris Biennale exhibition of contemporary art, creating exhibition spaces and selecting exhibitors.

What is astonishing is that all this turmoil produced some of the best contemporary projects and buildings in France, often against the odds. The temptation to let go, to settle for second best, to "keep the show on the road" must have been strong, but Nouvel never deviated from his purpose. The constant point in all these changes of structure has been Jean Nouvel's adherence to the qualities and values of his architecture. His commitment to his principles has been put severely to the test over the years, and continues to be in the new commercial world in which he is working, but his attitude remains unflinching—refreshed by an enormous personal *joie de vivre*. This is something I know personally: for several months in 1994 we worked together on the *International Design Year-*

Les Godets, Antony, France

OPPOSITE The theater at Belfort

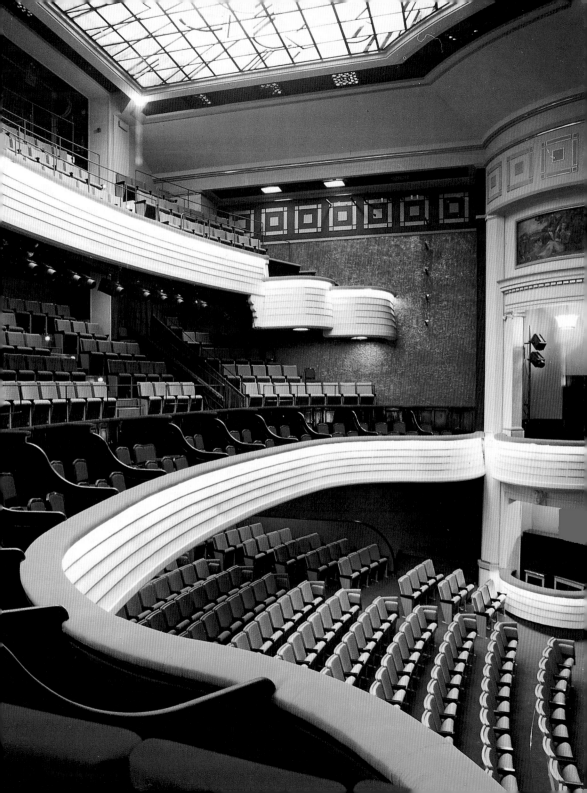

*book*, for which he was selector and I was general editor. Compared to everything else going on at the time, it was the most insignificant project imaginable, yet whenever we met it was the focus of his energy and attention. As he said in the interview cited above:

> It's true that I have an incredible desire to do things, to catch every opportunity, to upset the ordinary, the banal, the everyday. This desire is perhaps what makes me eager and determined. I love finding the limits of the possible, the edges of my knowledge and under-

standing. So when I decide on a project, my imagination fires up about the best ways of attaining it, the best strategy to take, and my time rushes past until I have found a solution.... The job of being an architect never leaves me any peace: I try to get away from it in reading, the cinema, travel, and talking with friends about their interests. But I'm always caught out and dragged back to architecture—by the decor of a film, the subject of a book, the landscape of a country— even a friend's suggestion which I find myself immediately transposing into architectural terms!

La Coupole cultural center, Combs la Ville, France

Exhibition design for Les Années 50, Pompidou Center, Paris

"I began to consider the question of light at the Institut du Monde Arabe. The theme of light is reflected in the southern wall consisting entirely of camera shutters, in the stacking of the stairs, the blurring of contours, the super-impositions, reflections, and shadows."

Jean Nouvel,
Lecture in London, 1995

# Institut du Monde Arabe

PARIS, FRANCE

The Institut du Monde Arabe (IMA), won by Nouvel in competition in 1982 and opened five years later, was the project that lifted him from his role as an active polemicist in French architecture to the international status that he has since enjoyed. The building was conceived as a center and showcase for Arab culture in Paris, partly funded by the French government and partly by a number of different Arab states. It houses an exhibition area, library, restaurant, and meeting rooms, and has remained, despite certain vicissitudes in its internal fortunes, one of the most popular Parisian museums.

Many commentators have referred to Nouvel's "understanding of Arab architecture and culture" in his design. Certainly it is possible to draw parallels between elements of the IMA and traditional Arab buildings. Nouvel himself refers to the stream of water that was to run from the top floor down a 30-meter flight of steps as a *shaddar*, and compares the *moucharabiens*, the patterns of squares and polygons on the southern walls, to similar designs at the Alhambra in Toledo with Granada. But he himself points out that the IMA is not an Arab building but a Western one. It is not merely Western in terms of its location, but in the public it addresses (unlike, say, a contemporary mosque), and in its conception and

OPPOSITE The main entrance. The museum is in the northern wing (at left); the library and conference room are in the southern wing (at right).

ABOVE The interior lightwell, hung with thin sheets of white marble over the walls to create an effect of alabaster that lightens and darks with changes of light

function. The concept of a cultural center, which combines spaces for exhibitions, events, performances, conferences, and lectures with a library, cinema, and resource center, is not merely Western, it originates in France, with the program of provincial maisons de culture initiated in France by André Malraux when he was Minister of Culture under President de Gaulle. The grandest expression of this genre, also French, is the Pompidou Center in Paris.

The Institut is on a curving triangular site on the south (or left) bank of the Seine, upstream from the Île de la Cité in Paris. The north side faces a road running along the edge of the river; the east looks across an open paved area to the Brutalist-on-*piloti* buildings of the University of Jussieu, dull and depressing concrete slabs from the early 1960s. The axis of the entrance is on Notre Dame; the left wall is angled at 91 degrees to the entrance plane, to lock the vista. Thus, as Olivier Boissière has pointed out, it occupies a pivotal position between modern Paris—the Gaullist technocracy symbolized by Jussieu—and traditional Paris, with the Île de la Cité and its historic buildings.

ABOVE The Institut seen from across the Seine. The curve of the northern facade echoes the curve of the road and river beside it. The university buildings of Jussieu can be seen at the right.

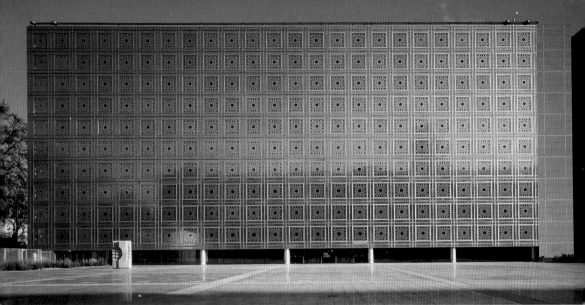

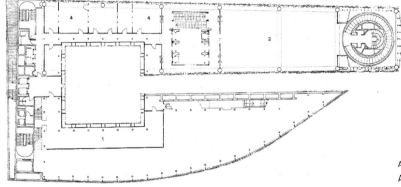

ABOVE The Institut du Monde
Arabe in evening light.

BELOW Plan for the seventh floor.
The open lightwell is in the center,
the angled entrace and the main-
staircase at top right.

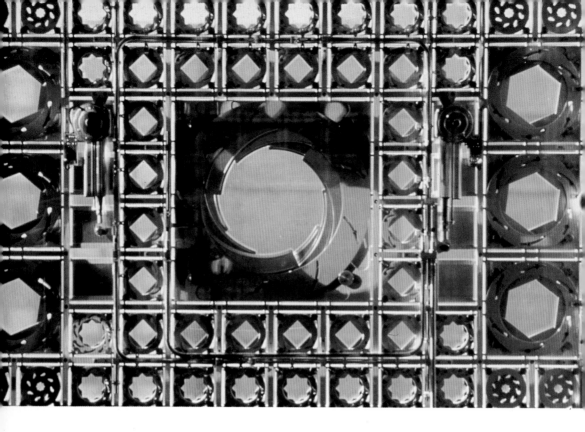

Nouvel's convictions about the function and duty of architecture provided the main impetus behind the design. Writing in 1986, the year before the building opened and with it in mind, he made the point that "a cultural position in architecture is a necessity. That involves refusing the use of ready-made or facile solutions, in order to permit an approach which is both global in its conception and specific to the site. . . . If the southern side of the building is a contemporary expression of Oriental culture, with the diaphragms, the northern is a literal mirror of Western culture, as images of the nearby Parisian cityscape have been enamelled on the exterior glass, like the passage of chemicals over a photographic plate. This pattern of line and marks on the same facade is also an echo of contemporary art. The frontiers between architecture, interior design, and product or furniture design are in my mind a total fiction. For that reason I designed the whole of the museum of the Institut, including the showcases, seating, and display furniture."

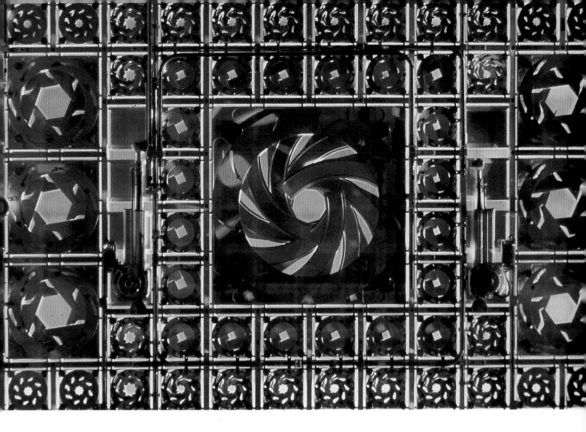

The IMA is not an Eastern building in Western materials: it is much subtler and more complex than that. It is a contemporary building, so it uses contemporary materials. It makes a series of precise statements about its location. It is a building about the organization and change of light in space—literally through the photosensitive motorized diaphragms on the south wall and the alabaster-hung light well in the center. In the interior, this translates into sudden changes of light levels, spatial volumes, and sensations of openness and closure. The building thrives on the contrasts and complexities it generates, an energy that makes visiting the building like walking through a film shot. "The sequences of changes," says Nouvel, "between different volumes and different light levels, according to different trajectories through it can be seen as a series of camera angles and apertures." It is certainly the design of his in which the relationship between architecture and cinema is closest and most satisfying.

The *moucharabiens* at the Institut, controlled by photoelectric cells to open and close in response to changing exterior light levels.

Light effects in the Institut, in
the main stairwell (opposite), the
library (above), and the elevator
bank (right).

"Functional markings form part of
my visual world. The Nemausus
housing I built in Nîmes reflected
my resolve to change the spirit of
council housing."

Jean Nouvel,
Lecture in Milan, 1995

# Nemausus Housing

NIMES, FRANCE

The Nemausus social housing project has, in the eleven years since
it was completed in 1987, become so well known (and even imi-
tated at times) that it is difficult to put its radical qualities into
proper perspective. The use of industrial materials (concertina
garage doors for balconies, metalwork decking, aluminum open
stairs) is indeed radical, but does not derive from any intention to
shock or to be radical for its own sake.

When Nouvel was asked in 1985 by Jean Bousquet, mayor of
Nîmes, to design a social housing project on the outskirts of the
city, Nouvel adopted his usual approach of analyzing the context
and content of the project to define a number of parameters from
which a solution could be generated. Among the key questions was
the definition of a "good" apartment. A good apartment was, quite
simply, as big an apartment as possible. A good apartment was
flexible, changeable. And a good apartment was inexpensive (the
rental prices were initially to be based on the construction costs).
That is the democratic aspect. Next the question of the site. Nîmes
is a town near the Mediterranean, with good weather for much of
the year and a tradition of living outdoors. The specific site was part
of what had been an arboretum, so some of the trees, particularly

OPPOSITE Exterior detail. The
word Nemausus comes from the
Roman name for the city's fresh-
water spring.

two lines of plane trees, running down the middle of the site, should be kept. The surrounding townscape is a mixture of low-level housing and light industry. That is the contextual aspect. The forms of the final project are derived from the parameters.

These parameters read back out of the finished project. Maximum apartment size was provided for by minimizing communal spaces such as stairways and halls (by putting the access stairs on the exterior, for example, and by providing each apartment with access to a wide balcony on each side). Flexibility was created by devising seventeen different modules for apartment layouts (one-room studio, split-level, tri-level, etc.) mixed into the 114 apartments contained in the two blocks. The low cost requirement was met by using prefabricated industrial elements for interior and exterior fittings (the building shell is thin concrete cased in aluminum sheeting). The balconies provide outdoor living to the full: full-depth concertina

doors allow the balcony to be completely integrated with the main living space. Plane trees separate the two blocks of buildings (one long, one short) and provide a changing screen of foliage with the seasons.

Nouvel's aesthetic intervention then comes into play. Markings such as the barber-pole stairway supports, the red bandings on the folding doors, or the simple dots of color on interior walls move away from a purely industrial metaphor and give the buildings their own independent personality, their *genus loci*. The buildings have as a result both a presence and an absence: it is clear from the bicycles and laundry, glimpsed through the metal meshwork of the balconies, that they are habitations, but they look as if they could not possibly be there and yet could not be anywhere else.

Social housing projects are seen by some as the Achilles' heel of contemporary architecture: endless new ideas met by endless failures, fated to become the visual evidence of urban decay. The Nemausus project, as Nouvel is the first to admit, would not have been possible but for the positive support of Jean Bousquet throughout the whole process. The French administration won out

OPPOSITE The industrial decking used on the balconies allows light to flow through at all times

ABOVE The two Nemausus buildings in their context of low-level housing, on the outskirts of the city

ABOVE Detail of the balconies and
stairs, showing the use of inexpensive industrial materials

OPPOSITE View toward the city
center from the top-floor balconies

OVERLEAF Interior views of one
studio apartment, showing the full-
length folding garage doors to the
balcony (left) and the metalwork
stairs (right)

in the end, by charging rents based on floor area, pushing the
larger apartments out of the hands (or pockets) of those for whom
they had been intended. The originality and innovation of the buildings, when completed, drew much comment, some of it unfavorable.
The best judgment of the building perhaps comes from its users, the
people who live there. There is a strong community enthusiasm for
the unusual apartments, and in some cases, for example, families
will occupy several apartments, as children who grow up leave the
parental home, but are determined to stay in a building which they
are proud of and enjoy.

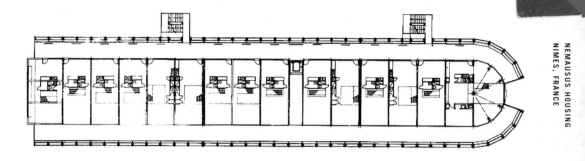

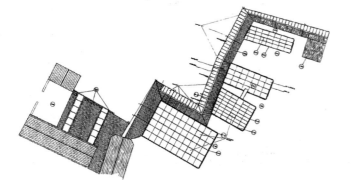

"The discovery of a new recipe does more for the happiness of the human race than the discovery of a new star."

Anthelme Brillat-Savarin

# Hôtel St. James

BOULIAC, FRANCE

For Anthelme Brillat-Savarin, the eighteenth-century gastronome, "the host is responsible for his guest for all the time the guest is with him." When the restaurateur Jean-Marie Amat at Bouliac, near Bordeaux, called on Jean Nouvel to extend his restaurant and build a small hotel, he perhaps had this precept in mind. Nouvel's solution certainly integrates the two elements, while conceding the individual integrity of the guest—no two room plans in the hotel are the same, for example. Also, respecting the sentiment of Brillat-Savarin, if not two centuries of grand *hôtellerie*, the hotel rooms are sparse and simple, focusing attention on the delights of the land-scape and the food. In the bedrooms the beds are relatively high, giving a view through the windows. The hotel is in a tiny village, near a square-towered church, and looks out over the vineyards of the Garonne valley.

The hotel consists of four small buildings, at most three stories high. The Hôtel St. James is a rarity among Nouvel's projects, in that it is not placed in a dense urban setting. Instead, the facades of the buildings create a density of their own. The interiors have plain concrete floors and waxed plaster walls: no moldings or dec-oration. The ample windows are framed in grey metal, also used for

ABOVE Overall plan, showing the relationship of the four build-ings that comprise the hotel and restaurant

OPPOSITE View from one building of the hotel toward the restaurant, showing the light effect created by the external perforated metal sheeting

113

The four buildings of the hotel
from the adjacent vineyard. The
external covering, which is
intended to weather and rust over
time, resembles that of tobacco-
drying sheds found in the area.

cladding unwindowed areas. Beyond these are metal grilles, some fixed, some mobile, which can be raised or tilted to admit the light and the view. This layering is also appreciated from the exterior. The outer grilles have a deliberate rusted color (reminiscent of the tobacco-drying sheds found in the region) which is revealed beneath the texture and color of the grey cladding or glass giving onto the stripped interiors. The exterior shapes of the buildings are traditional, comprising simple roofs without eaves, or in one case, a flat roof terrace. This "fractal vision," in Olivier Boissière's phrase, is all the stronger for being encapsulated in such a small frame.

The original work on the Hôtel St. James, done between 1987 and 1989, included the creation of the eighteen-bedroom hotel and redesign of the restaurant, and the design of the "Bistroy" bistro, intended for a younger clientele and housed in the former cold store, a fact recorded in the decoration of the space. Since then, Nouvel has returned to design an outdoor eating area, the brasserie, and the swimming pool, which is black. For the brasserie the vertical grilles become horizontal sunshades, with a simple white cloth hung below them to shield the guests from direct light. One side is open along its length; along the other, stone columns are covered with climbing plants.

ABOVE LEFT Nouvel designed the guest-room furniture for the hotel

ABOVE RIGHT The simple beds with adjustable headboards are raised to accommodate the view and subtly refer to the regional tradition of high country beds.

OPPOSITE The open-air brasserie (above) and the surrounding countryside as seen from a hotel bedroom (below).

Nouvel designed the chairs and tables for the hotel. From basic principles "What should a chair be? A seat and legs, a back and arms, is enough"—he created simple, round cushioned shapes mounted on chrome pipe work, with plain white covers, which could be removed easily for cleaning. The furniture looks slightly frail, but has an air of sophisticated simplicity that is in keeping with the building and its site. This simplicity is not "Petit-Trianonisme," playing at being in the country while enjoying the best of food and wine; it is more honest than that. It is a way of creating a framework in which what is offered —the landscape and the menu —can be enjoyed calmly and without disruption.

"I wanted the Opera House to seem like a beating heart. In the interior I wanted to juxtapose two systems. I kept the original gold in the foyer and treated all the new floors in black granite, polished like a mirror."

Jean Nouvel,
Lecture in Milan, 1995

# Opera House

LYON, FRANCE

"Lyon a un Nouvel Opera" (Lyon has a new opera, or Lyon has an opera by Nouvel), the posters on the Lyon subway read in 1993, when the building opened, making a simple pun on Nouvel's name, which means "new" in French. The competition to extend and renovate the Opera House in Lyon, the second largest city in France, was won by Nouvel in 1986 with a project that used the old building, particularly its grand ground- and first-floor facades on the south, east, and west, as a point of departure and reference for the new. The brief called for providing a larger auditorium, a second 200-seat amphitheater (which Nouvel placed in the three new basement levels) and public spaces, including a restaurant, new rehearsal facilities, and a fly tower.

By retaining the older facades, Nouvel linked the building to the surrounding official buildings, such as the adjacent nineteenth-century Hôtel de Ville, the town hall and mayor's office for the city, and the nearby City Museum, housed in the nineteenth-century Palais de Saint Pierre. The new drum roof, like the lid of an enormous jewel box, however, marks it as wholly contemporary. This contradiction resolves itself, since the balance between the two elements is matched by their contrast, in material, texture, and color.

ABOVE Main facade of the Opera House, showing the original ground floor and *piano nobile*, which Nouvel retained, and the new drum roof

OPPOSITE The dark and lustrous shapes of the main hall can be seen in the circulation spaces

**119**

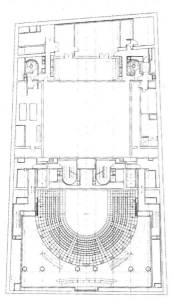

An artifice, perhaps, but what is the essence of theater but artifice? New glass walls or glazed entrances have been inserted between arches of the old colonnades, so that from within and without the grey-black lustrous underside of the new main auditorium appears suspended in the 30-meter-high vault of the entry hall. A series of escalators, metalwork stairways, and suspended walkways takes the public up to the entry levels of the main hall. The lighting in this space is clear and soft, as so often in Nouvel's buildings, and again the interior is visible from the exterior, especially at street level. Within the entrance hall, which runs the full width of the building, the reflections off the curving shell of the auditorium, glass walling, and dark polished floor, together with the contours of the suspended mass, which at times is hardly more than seven feet from the floor, create a complex, ambiguous, and inviting space of a different poetic order than the street life outside.

The entry to the actual auditorium is through short corridors, with double doors for soundproofing, and bathed in red light to create a complete contrast between the dark, mysterious architecture outside and the more grandiose interior of the hall. A similar contrast is found in the public foyers, where in one case, the main bar, the original ceiling and fittings have been restored in all their gilt splendor, but with a modern mirrored floor. In the auditorium itself each

OPPOSITE Downtown Lyon, with the Opera House and its adjoining pedestrian plaza at center

ABOVE (LEFT) Plan of the main auditorium level

ABOVE (RIGHT) The entry passages to the main auditorium are lit in red.

121

seat back is fitted with a small light fed from a fiber-optic cable. This technological innovation evolved from the eighteenth century, when theaters had candleholders in each seat back to illuminate the faces of the audience. Red light bathes the exterior at night, particularly under the drum of the arch enclosing the new rehearsal rooms, behind and above the peristyle of the facade. By both night and day this dense and complex building forms a new landmark for the city.

The rehearsal room sits under the top of the grey steel-and-glass arch that marks the new construction. Actors and musicians, singers and dancers can look down the main pedestrian street of the city from the window that runs across the whole elevation. It might have been tempting to put a public space there, such as a restaurant, and bury the rehearsal rooms in a basement. But in a sense, if Lyon is to have a new opera, the opera has to have Lyon as well.

OPPOSITE The Opera House at night, with the rehearsal area in use

ABOVE (LEFT) The statues of the muses, now lit in red, were retained from the original facade.

ABOVE (RIGHT) The rehearsal area under the main roof vault. Colored lights illuminate the space at night.

OVERLEAF The seatback lights that gently illuminate the audience's faces can be seen in this photograph of the main auditorium in use.

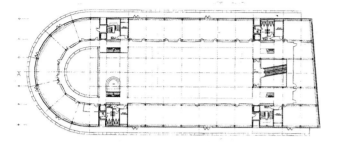

"Philippe Michel had a vision of a post-industrial society preparing for a 'civilization of the person.' The building he commissioned me to create was to incorporate this dimension."

Jean Nouvel,
Lecture in Milan, 1995

# CLM/BBDO

ISSY-LES-MOULINEAUX, FRANCE

Issy-les-Moulineaux is located south of the river Seine at the south-western extremity of Paris. It is a border area, which at one time had a military presence (the Fort d'Issy was a properly Vaubanesque pentagon) and later service industries and warehousing along road and river for the city beyond. On the northern edge of Issy-les-Moulineaux, between two branches of the Seine, is the Île St. Germain. Old Parisian plans mark "subsistances militaires" as covering its upstream half, but they were cleared a decade or more ago, when the area was under consideration as a potential site for a Paris World's Fair. The plan came to nothing, but drew the interest of design companies and architects to the area. So when the late Philippe Michel, head of the CLM/BBDO advertising agency, decided that he wanted to build a new office, he chose Issy-les-Moulineaux as the site and Jean Nouvel as his architect.

The Île St. Germain is a strangely mixed area: on the far side of the Seine a motorway approach road rumbles over its *pilotis*, and in the river itself barges and boats are moored, some abandoned, some inhabited. On the land, small wooden cottages in need of paint stand next to a car wrecker's yard, or a smart new school, or a trim modern home. A hundred meters away from the CLM/BBDO site,

OPPOSITE The prow of the building sits in a small artificial lake planted with water weeds.

Philippe Starck's offices are housed in a pistachio-painted metal shed next to his Le Moult house, a miniature concrete ziggurat. Five hundred meters away is a dull modern office block. For the architect, it was a site with no contextual references at all—or perhaps too many. For the client, who wanted his agency to be unique, it was an opportunity to mark out a special territory.

The result is as quirky and complex as the area in which it is located. It has been described by Olivier Boissière as "an old rusting freighter" with an oyster's interior, and by Patrice Goulet as a shipwreck in an aquatic garden. The external appearance of the building is intriguing: the rounded, rust-stained prow resting in the water; the entry deck like a marine loading bay; the profile of the closed roof like battened hatches; the purposeful catwalks running along the sides. It sits somber and squat against the riverside junk. Inside, light, color, and steel make a deliberate and exciting contrast: floors of jigsaw-patterned metal mesh in the offices, solid red leather seating, ceiling lights behind frosted and screenprinted glass with aluminum foil backing. To understand the logic of the design— the qualities that take it beyond pastiche to a redefinition of office space—one must start with the interior.

Philippe Michel, who tragically died before the building was completed, believed that communication and creativity were the business of his business, and that an advertising agency only worked if the flow of ideas and concepts was unfettered. Play, casual contact, informality: these were as important as hierarchy or formal structure. The form of the interior emerged from his discussing these ideas with Nouvel. At the main floor level there is an atrium, ten meters deep by fifteen wide and twenty long, with three floors of offices and rooms arranged around it, crossed by metal gangways. At one end of the atrium is a bar, with decor by the American artist Gary Glaser. The large seats, designed by Nouvel, are in red leather: "like a punching bag," he points out, "and designed to be sat or leaned on, with a broad back for putting down papers for a moment, in a passing meeting." The rooms have windows to the interior, which create contact and access. On the walkways linking

11|20

OPPOSITE Interior of the main office space

OVERLEAF The building at night with its immense roof panels open

the offices above the atrium, the safety barriers are topped by broad red leather slabs, to lean or sit on, or to meet by.

"Michel wanted to maximize the opportunities for encounters, for contact," Marie-Thérése Baldran, the construction-phase architect, explains. "People aren't necessarily creative just sitting at a desk — they might want to work in the bar area, or share an idea at once with a passing colleague. Everything was arranged around the principle of freedom of movement. For example, the account managers would be as often at the client's office as at CLM/BBDO. So their desk at the home office was like a traveler's trunk that would close when not in use. 'Nomads don't need fixed furniture,' Michel used to say."

This concept of mobility led to the metaphor of a boat for the exterior appearance — not a yacht or liner, but a working boat, low in the water under its load, moored to the shore, surrounded by water

weeds ("We deliberately planted weeds, not flowers," says Baldran), rough and rugged outside, open and efficient within. To crown the concept of openness, the roof opens, like the shell of an oyster. In fact there are two systems of roof openings that transform the lighting and sense of space of the interior: the individual skylights open, as do four huge roof panels, each seven by eight meters in size, lifted by a mechanism devised for lock gates.

The CLM/BBDO building is great fun, but it is serious fun. The focus on contact and efficiency in the interior space, rather than formal planning, and the design of furniture and decoration, point to a new definition of office function. This is appropriate for a creative communications business, but the principles set out here go further and could be applied more widely. Work is understood to be a social activity, requiring open spaces, opportunities to interact, points of exchange, and places for private thought or formal discourse.

OPPOSITE View across the interior of the main floor

ABOVE The main atrium

# Da Vinci Conference Center

TOURS, FRANCE

The inhabitants of Tours refer to their conference center, which opened in 1993, as *la casquette* (the cap), after its curved and projecting sunroof. This was a gift to the local political cartoonists. But the building is a cap in another sense: it caps the square onto which it opens, adding to the whole. The distinctive feature of the building, seen from photographs, is in a way deceptive. As the photographer Philippe Ruault explains, "To understand this building you have first to look at the site, at what the building has around it, in particular the Préfecture building and the railway station on the other sides of the square, and the gardens on the other side of the building. Concentrating on the building leads you to overlook how it is integrated into the site."

The question of integration was one of the first Nouvel addressed when planning the project, won in an invited competition in 1989. "The constraints of the site are both numerous and powerful," he wrote at the time, "and risk leading to a fixed, almost precast solution. All our work on the context of the place du Général Leclerc and the adjoining streets was to avoid the fatal temptation to give in to the site, producing a bit of architectural accompaniment, rather than a real building." Among the constraints were limita-

OPPOSITE The main entrance at night

ABOVE General view, showing how the building fits into the angled corner of the square

planta auditorios
cote - 1.40
audiorio plan
level + 3.40

tions on the height of the building relative to its surroundings, the existing street-plan, and the position of the building between an urban square and a public garden. The building therefore had to have presence without monumentality; it had to both act as a passageway between square and park and to provide functional interior spaces. The 20,000-square-meter site was to hold three concert halls, seating 2,000, 800, and 400, respectively.

Nouvel placed the three concert halls in line along the spine of the building, with the largest at the back and the smallest at the front; the service tower was also located at the very back. Because of the slope of the site, the floor of the largest concert hall is one story below ground level. The location of the building also suggested the creation of unencumbered views through it, especially at ground level. This would both show passersby the park on the other side and give a glimpse of the activity within, and thus extend an invitation to enter and share. The concert halls are suspended on cantilevered beams, a piece of engineering that Frédérique Mejanes, the job architect, describes as one of the most exciting aspects of the project. As a result, there is a clear view under and around the curving underhang of the two smaller halls, finished on the exterior with anthracite grey metal. Following this principle of transparency, the escalators and stairs that link the floors with the entrances to the concert halls are clear: the works of the building become self-evident, both within and without. This is carried through all the lateral levels, so that the access passages around the upper levels of the halls give onto either the square or the park, depending on the side of the building, while the end wall of the trade exhibition area, under the roof, is glazed floor to ceiling, allowing for an unbroken view of the station across the square.

OPPOSITE (ABOVE) The adjoining public garden is clearly visible from the open spaces on the ground floor.

OPPOSITE (BELOW) The main public area below the auditorium. As these two images demonstrate, Nouvel prefers low, side-lit public areas to the more conventional atrium.

ABOVE Plan showing the three auditoriums in line

At dusk or at night, this transparency takes on a new form. The walls framing the forward part of the building, internally and externally, are fitted with horizontal lines of colored fluorescent tubes behind frosted glass. These create lines or squares of color (depending on the viewer's distance) within and without the building at street level, which are reflected on the dark curved masses of the hall shells and on the polished floors. The result is both mysterious and compelling at first sight, and ordered, once it is analyzed; it reiterates the tension, complexity, and power of the building in daylight.

There are similarities in the treatment of the shell of the concert halls with Nouvel's work at Lucerne (page 26), where the shell is covered in wooden veneer with deep red edging, and at the Opera House in Lyon (page 118), where the shell is finished in a lustrous grey-black. In all three structures the shell is visible both from the stalls seating and from under the roof of the building. But to see this as a Nouvel hallmark would be wrong. The solution in each case arises from the overall conception of the individual building, not from some existing ideology or mental pattern book. At Tours, the arrangement of the halls was dictated partly by the requirements of the roofline, partly by the knowledge that a monumental building would be inappropriate. The arrangement of the halls in turn suggested a cantilevered structure in suspension, so clearing the space beneath for lateral views at different levels became a major requirement from Nouvel's point of view. Part of the pleasure of this building lies in the way its structural logic integrates flawlessly with its functional logic, as well as its placement in the urban fabric.

Nouvel himself sees Tours as a paradox: "a paradox between external simplicity and internal complexity, between the compact and the transparent, between symmetry and diversity, in its response to the street and the gardens. What I hope is that this thread of contradictions makes the da Vinci Conference Center both natural and evident: a building made to be where it is."

OPPOSITE (ABOVE) Detailed of the colored fluorescent lighting in the foyer

OPPOSITE (BELOW) Interior view toward the entrance at night. The colored neon striplights change in appearance according to the viewer's angle of approach.

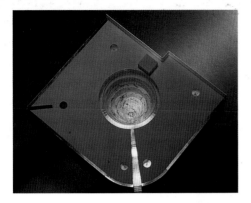

"The concepts of light, of depth, of stressing the commercial aspects by means of signs, recur in the Galeries Lafayette building."

Jean Nouvel,
Lecture in Milan, 1995

# Galeries Lafayette

BERLIN, GERMANY

Before World War II, before the Communists came in and the Wall went up, the Friedrichstrasse was a fashionable street in central Berlin; unfortunately, it was in the eastern part of the city. After the reunification of Germany, city authorities, together with commercial developers, staged a competition for rebuilding three adjacent sites on the street. I.M. Pei and Oswald Ungers were awarded two of the projects. The third, on the corner, appropriately enough, of Franzosichstrasse ("French Street") was won by Nouvel. It was to be a mixed-use building, with 10 percent housing, 15 percent offices, and the rest allocated to commercial use; Galeries Lafayette had expressed an interest in creating a department store at that location, which was confirmed after the competition.

The corner site posed the problem of linking the adjacent facades, which was resolved by turning the corner between them through a series of arcs. In the original proposal, a long V-shaped glazed section running from the corner to the center was to be inserted through the whole depth of the building, roof to ground floor. This idea of opening the shop to the street was later set aside on grounds of cost and wasted space (as one of the job architects said, "The construction company was also one of the investors in the project,

ABOVE The original model for the project, showing the V-shaped lighting slot through the building

OPPOSITE View from the Friedrichstrasse

which gave site meetings a different slant!"). A similar concept was retained in the interior, where conical light-wells cut through the office levels of the building down to the first floor. This motif is repeated, literally in reverse, in the store area, where a large interior cone functions both as a light-well and as a point of reference for shoppers.

The cones also function as an emblem for the building. Because the street level has an entirely glazed exterior, people passing by have a clear view into it. More subtly, the interior surfaces of the main upward cone are used as a projection screen. In conventional anamorphosis, distorted images are restored to correct perspective by being projected onto curved or conical surfaces. Here the opposite is true: "correct" images are distorted by the curved surface. Through this swirl of color the shopper can see the other floors of the store. At night, large panels and strips on the exterior facades at store level become screens for displaying images and messages. Thus both exterior and interior become a projection, a whirling pattern of luminous dots, a metaphor for the flow of information and sensation, the permanent state of change that is central, in Nouvel's view, to the modern urban experience.

The cones in the commercial area are also a reinterpretation of the immense skylights that were a feature of the first department store, the Bon Marché in Paris; those skylights referred to the glazed arcades that housed earlier rows of shops. Bringing daylight into the shop area runs counter to current retail practice, where the shopper is cocooned from the exterior by the profusion of goods on display; often in refurbished shops upper-floor windows become

OPPOSITE Patterns of reflection in the glass lighting cones in the office area

ABOVE The entrance corner of the Galeries Lafayette

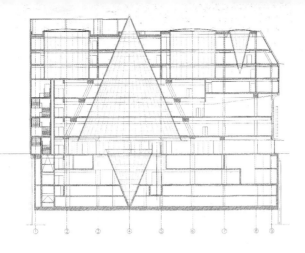

storage areas. Nouvel not only brings back light; through the projected images, such as logos and trademarks, he also reminds shoppers of the vortex of urban life that surrounds them, and which shopping is both a part of and an escape from.

Similar conical and cylindrical light-wells are also used in the office floors; plain glass cones and columns drop from the roof through the top four floors, providing natural light to offices away from the periphery of the building. The circular spaces around the cones at different floor levels serve as passageways and communal areas for formal or informal meetings. A working dynamic is thus built into the pattern of office life through the play of different and original spaces (some offices even have part of a light-well as a wall); the uniform or modular boxes used in so many space planning projects are much more static. Both the commercial area and the office spaces were delivered as shell and core, so the interior design work by Nouvel was otherwise confined to communal areas such as entrances and elevators.

The Galeries Lafayette project was one of Nouvel's first major designs for a non-French client, and working with a different set of planning and construction regulations posed a number of problems. Quite apart from the loss of the glazed entrance that featured in the original design, the external signage is not as prominent in reality as on the proposal. The dark curves of the building seem somber, as if meditating on the complex and tormented history of Berlin in the twentieth century.

OPPOSITE The central lighting cone gives shoppers and visitors a range of views through the building.

ABOVE Section drawing, showing lighting cones for the retail area and lightwells for the offices

"The immaterial caught in a grid is the theme here. The tree planted by Chateaubriand is a real historical monument. That is why the architecture endeavors to emphasize it, to frame it."

Jean Nouvel,
Lecture in Milan, 1995

# Fondation Cartier

PARIS, FRANCE

Passing the Cartier building on the Boulevard Raspail, even the most impatient Parisian taxi drivers slow down to take a look. It is one of the most simple yet exciting and intriguing buildings in the city, and rapidly became a landmark after it opened in 1994.

This building for Cartier does not represent Nouvel's first involvement with the company. He had designed a factory for them in Switzerland some years before, and was the company president's immediate choice as architect when the future of the Fondation Cartier came under review. The foundation has a strong reputation in France, particularly for their exhibitions of work by young contemporary artists. For many years it was located in Poussec, south of Paris. Jean Nouvel, together with the specialist museum architect Jean-François Bodin, put forward a proposal for a new building which incorporated an office tower. The site was a sloping one, and the design showed entrances to the museum and offices at the top of the slope along a horizontal walkway to the top of the office tower. This proposal failed to convince the planning authorities.

When the site in the Boulevard Raspail become vacant—it had previously been the American Cultural Center—Cartier took a lease on

OPPOSITE The historic tree of liberty planted by Chateaubriand, which is the focus of the Fondation Cartier building

ABOVE Site plan, showing the relationship of the building to street

the site with the intention of moving the Fondation to the city center and establishing their head office for France there. They stipulated that Nouvel was to be the architect. The site contained a historic "Tree of Liberty" planted by Chateaubriand some 200 years before, set in a garden behind a wall. Any new project needed to respect these elements, as well as meet with the approval of a strong local residents committee.

With projects such as the Tour Sans Fins and the Tokyo Opera House, Nouvel had already been studying the question of transparency and opacity. As he says, "I believe in a Darwinism of architecture, in relation to materials. Not in the sense that materials will somehow disappear, but that our technology of materials, and so our control over materiality, will increase and improve so that we will need less and less material to do a specific task. One of the main ways of controlling material is through light, and so one of the most astonishingly modern materials, in this sense, the most evolved, is glass." The site, with its tree and garden, and the functions of the building—part exhibition area, part offices— suggested glass architecture would be appropriate. Nouvel's solution was a simple nine-story glass box, twice as long as it is deep, parallel to the Boulevard Raspail. The exhibition area is a clear, double-floor space on the ground and first floors, broken only by a central mezzanine. Further exhibition space is located in the basement, and the offices would be on the upper floors. The main entrance would be central, under the mezzanine, flanking the famous tree, with a elevator to access the car park to the right. In plan and organization of space, this is wholly sensible and straightforward. Executed with a maximum of glass and a minimum of grey steel, the building has three additional features that transform it from a plain glazed block into a series of overlapping transparent layers. First, the wall onto the street, some 15 meters in front of the main facade, has been replaced by a glass wall 18 meters high with minimal grey steel framing. Second, glazed walls at the front and back of the building project 10 meters in each direction beyond the side walls. And third, the 8.5-meter-high main exhibition spaces are completely glazed. The result is a building almost wholly trans-

The Fondation Cartier seen from across the Boulevard Raspail in evening light

parent, framing the tree and the surrounding garden between the exterior glass wall and the receding planes of the building itself.

"I sometimes wonder if I'm seeing the building or the image of the building, if Cartier is about transparency or about reflection," Nouvel says. Whichever it is, it completely validates the emphasis he places on the importance of light: weather, time of day, angle of view, relative levels of interior and exterior lighting—all conspire to create new images and patterns. The central office area is generally denser than the rest, though the interior walls are in sandblasted glass, so the building is never fully opaque.

The idea of an exhibition area with transparent walls seems problematic: how can the visitor engage with the work when the garden and the traffic can be clearly seen all around? In addition, the glass panels are also doors, so the whole of the ground-level space can be opened physically to the exterior, for example for an installation by lighting designer Ingo Maurer, who planted several thousand small luminous colored tubes in the garden and gallery. Other exhibitions, such as Ron Arad's collection of curving, highly polished tables, actually benefited from the play of reflections from the outside. However, the design of the gallery space is not merely a matter of the architect's whim, nor is it justified by the fact that certain exhibitions profit from it, or that there is a suite of standard exhibition spaces in the basement level with museum-quality lighting and environmental controls. Rather, the design stems from Nouvel's view that the conventional museum or gallery approach is outmoded. "Art needs to be experienced more widely," he once said, "not through schemes of patronage like the .01% idea, but by a greater public involvement. And the definitions of art are changing continually: the space at Cartier is designed to be entirely flexible. For one exhibition it can be draped, for another open. It can be partitioned, and lit in different ways."

OPPOSITE (ABOVE) On the open top deck, successive layers of glass combine to produce reflections

OPPOSITE (BELOW) Inside or outside? Building or reflection? In the offices on the upper floors, sandblasted glass is used to divide spaces.

ABOVE Installation by the artist Jean-Michel Alberola in the ground-floor gallery

# Competitions

Nouvel's approach to architecture, with its insistence on the specificity of the site, is perhaps ideally suited to competition work, and competitions are a way for a young architect to get ideas published and publicized, if not built. As a competition winner, competition loser (very often), and now as a competition juror (for the World Bank building in Washington, and the Bastille Opera House in Paris, for example), Nouvel's main concern is not with the fairness of competitions, but with their appropriateness. "Imagine," he asks, "holding a competition to write a novel! How would you decide between publishing Umberto Eco or Gabriel Garcia Marquez? Often on a jury I find two or three projects that are equally valid as approaches to the task. A jury isn't therefore always the best way to decide how to go. The best situation is a competition win together with a client who supports the project, as at Tours or Lyon for us. Or, as now we are more widely recognized, a direct approach from a client, which is itself a first mark of confidence."

Photomontage of the Tour
Sans Fins project, next to the
Grande Arche de la Défense,
looking toward the center of
Paris

Nouvel's architecture is known both from his built work and from his competition projects, and no study of his achievement would be complete without some of these "lost opportunities."

# Tours Sans Fins

PARIS, FRANCE

"We still get people ringing us up and saying that they have been to La Défense and can't see the Tour Sans Fins," says Françoise Raynaud, who worked with Nouvel on the project. "George Fessy's photomontage is so good people believe it's an actual photograph, and a couple of books talk of the project as if it is built." There is a certain irony in this—after all, should a glass tower be visible, even if it does exist? Another reminder of the ambiguities of contemporary imagery is the building's appearance in a sequence in Wim Wenders's 1991 film *Until the End of the World*, an elegant compliment from the filmmaker to his friend Nouvel.

The Tour Sans Fins was the winning project in a 1988 competition for a site adjacent to the Grande Arche de la Défense. Nouvel's idea was to build a circular glass-walled tower that would become more transparent the higher it got: an unremarkable building and a complete contradiction to the accepted principle of the skyscraper, which relies, whatever style it is designed in, on presence so as to be artistically considered.

The project was to be financed by the Caisse de Dêpots, the largest bank in France, which acts both as banker to the French government and as an independent investment bank on major projects. The Tour would serve as a world trade center offering prestigious offices to French and international companies with no base in the capital itself. For this reason, Raynaud points out, detailed engineering studies and analyses were carried out to satisfy the investors of the feasibility of the project and the budget: it is ready to build. With the economic recession of the late 1980s, and consequent drops in office rents, the project became economically unfeasible. This is a sad reminder of Nouvel's frequent assertion that the future—and present—of modern cities is shaped by forces other than architecture and planning.

Model of the Tour Sans Fins

# Tokyo Opera House

TOKYO, JAPAN

On the skyline as you approach, it is a black, polished mirror monolith with curving sides and profile; "a whale that has swallowed the
*Ka'aba,*" Philippe Starck, who designed the interior furniture and
fittings, called it. Before it, through a low, wide entrance, ten meters
thick in grey-black granite, you walk into a black hall, polished
granite on all sides. In the distance there is a sudden line of light, a
bank of stairs and escalators rising through the three floors in a
single sweep into the main lobby. There, hovering above, are massive, distant, curved golden shapes, and before you a window thirty
meters high in the western wall; the seats in the main auditorium
are still a further ten meters above that. That is what the Tokyo
Opera House would have been like, had it won the 1986 competition. It was to be situated on a vacant lot in an amorphous, sprawl-
ing suburb of Tokyo, and to be used for productions of all kinds of
musical theater, except Japanese opera.

The Tokyo project can be read as a musical instrument case, a mirror, or a monument. Its inherent ambiguity is its essential quality:
like a mirror it reflects what is before it, but has its own existence
as well (as Magritte has pointed out). It would have been a building of profound subtlety, and on an immense scale. "If there is a literary reference here," Nouvel points out, "it is to Tanizaki's book
on shadows, and the idea he discusses of the *toko no ma,* the central dark space of an interior, in which the colors of bronze, lacquer,
or jade glow softly."

The scale aspect is not often realized, as the project is best known
through the small model produced for the competition. The model
opens to show the golden hulks of the three theaters set within it,
their vaguely cruciform shapes required by the fly towers, under-
stage machinery, and backstage facilities. The building would have
stood 80 meters high and been over 140 meters long by 70 wide.
Some whale, some *Ka'aba*!

ABOVE Exterior drawings of the
Tokyo Opera House

# Tête Défense

LA DÉFENSE, FRANCE

The most grandiose of President Mitterand's *grands projets*—perhaps also the most Hausmannian—was the virtual prolongation of the historic line of the Louvre, the Place de la Concorde, and the Champs Elysées across and beyond Paris itself, and to match the Arc de Triomphe with a new monument at La Défense. This made economic sense: there was no more room within Paris, particularly for large-scale office development, and the creation of the new axis into the growing business quarter of La Défense would give the area a direction and a link to the city. This expansion of the normally jealously guarded boundaries of Paris has had one odd side effect: Eurodisney has now been renamed Disneyland Paris, though it is miles from the city.

Nouvel's 1993 project for the Tête Défense competition posed the question of how to define by closure one of the best-known perspectives in the world. His answer: "By the sky, or rather by skies. Architectural ones. The sky is a canvas which is always being repainted. Its structure remains visible, like the squaring up of Old Master paintings." Nouvel planned to use the structure of the building to square up the sky, creating a central openwork grid with two blocks of office floors suspended at each side. With changes of sunlight and time of day, the grid would become by turns opaque or transparent, dark or golden, an effect illustrated by photographing the model against the setting sun.

Johann-Otto Spreckelsen's more architectural enclosure won the competition, but one can imagine what Nouvel's building might have resembled by looking across Tokyo Bay to the new FGC Headquarters Building by Kenzo Tange, which echoes both Nouvel's design and a permanent sun.

OPPOSITE (ABOVE) The model for the Tête Défense project, photographed against the setting sun

OPPOSITE (BELOW) AND ABOVE Details of the model

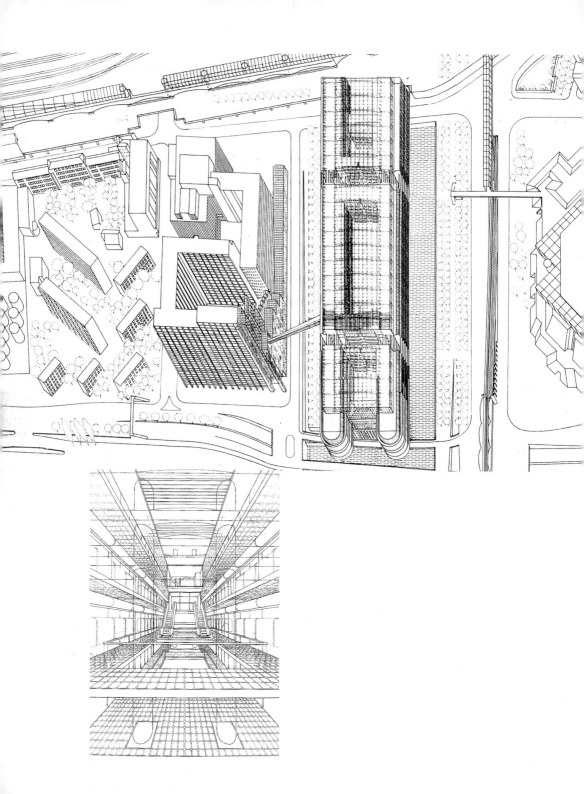

# Ministère des Finances

PARIS, FRANCE

For once, money gave way to art. The main office of the French Ministry of Finance was for years situated in the northwest wing of the Louvre, but the creation of Le Grand Louvre, begun with I.M. Pei's pyramid and concluded with the opening of the Richelieu wing, also designed by Pei, meant that the Ministry had to move. A site on the north bank of the Seine at Bercy, opposite the site of the future national library, was chosen. The competition to design the building on this narrow site, opening onto the river at one end and the railyards of Bercy at the other, was held in 1982.

Nouvel realized that the site marked not only a transition along the long axis, but also along the shorter one, from office buildings to the west and a more open area to the east. His proposal therefore included a long basin to the east of the building and a shorter one to the south, which would connect the building to the river: the long, low project, twelve stories high, was like a boat moored to a quay. Nouvel envisioned placing the offices against the external walls, in three blocks, raised on *pilotis*, leaving large central atriums in each. The northernmost one would also be built over the existing historic Customs House.

"This architectural exercise," he wrote at the time, "is part of a redefinition of the principles of the administrative building. Symbolically such a building must be transparent and open (as well as solid and protecting). Access to it must be clear, its organization simple, circulation within it well lit and signposted. The tools of the modern movement — *pilotis*, lighting, structural efficiency to liberate space, glazed external skin walls — are here exploited to the maximum in a horizontal statement which of itself overcomes the visual repetition of individual elements."

ABOVE Axonometric drawing

BELOW Interior perspective of the project

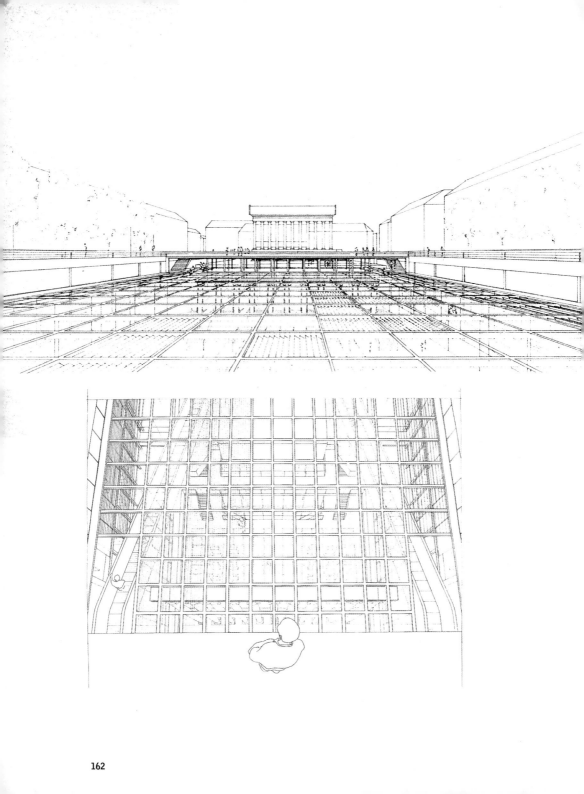

# Médiathèque

NIMES, FRANCE

Cleopatra's loss was Nîmes's gain. After she and Mark Antony were defeated in the first century B.C., the victor, Octavian, who later named himself the Emperor Augustus, rewarded his legionnaires with land around Nîmes and built for them public buildings, an arena, temples, and city walls. Nîmes, in western Provence, had long been inhabited because of an exceptional source of fresh water. The main temple was built in front of this famous spring, the Nemausus. Another, which still stands and is one of the finest surviving early Roman temples, is today called the Maison Carrée, and contains a museum of antiquities. The Médiathèque was to be on a site facing this small but elegant classical building.

Most of the proposals, including the winning one by Sir Norman Foster, involved mirroring the Maison Carrée with a freestanding building symmetrical to it. Not so Nouvel. He proposed a horizontal mirror, a sheet of spring water, and put the Médiathèque underneath it. The visitors would see the facade of the Maison Carrée reflected in the rectangular pool, and through the pool see down into the center. As they descended into the building itself, which would be toplit through the glass floor of the pool, they would pass through the archaeological strata of the city's history. Certain factors—location and function—underpin this solution. The city is an archaeological and historical site; it owes its original prosperity to the underground spring. As to the intended function, a media center is a virtual world, so putting the cybernauts into an archaeological space was a logical paradox.

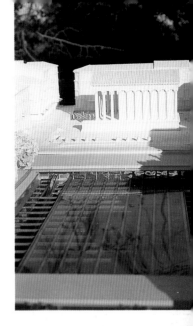

OPPOSITE Two perspective drawings for the Médiathèque, showing the submerged building in relation to the Maison Carré

ABOVE The model for the project

# Seine Rive Gauche

PARIS, FRANCE

The Seine Rive Gauche project concerned the redevelopment of both the railway yards behind the Gare d'Austerlitz, on the south bank of the Seine in eastern Paris, and the industrial areas of eastern Paris, including the Ministère des Finances on the northern bank, further upstream, and the new national library. The four L-shaped towers of Dominique Perrault's library, now appropriately renamed the Bibliothèque François Mitterand, later became a central landmark for this general restructuring.

Nouvel's proposal was to create what he called "Paris's Central Park," a riverside park that would provide much-needed green space for the surrounding residential areas. This would be achieved by placing the railway system underground and creating new facilities along the edge of the Seine. Some of these would be new buildings, some restorations of older ones. Nouvel's analysis revealed that the areas to the south and east of Austerlitz lacked any internal coherence and were cut off from the river by the railway. Integration, not wholesale rebuilding, was the key. Certain elements of the site, such as the station itself and one of the old warehouses on the river, were to be kept, and new building particularly hotels, cafés, and restaurants along the riverbank, would be planned to increase access and communication.

Nouvel's proposal, however, exceeded the site specified by the competition. His reasons were valid, but in the end his proposal was not chosen.

Sample documents from Nouvel's competition submission, demonstrating how Nouvel's combination of new and old elements would have appeared

166

# Baltic Tower

LONDON, ENGLAND

This project for an office block in London explores different volumes around a similar theme. Nouvel proposed four solutions as part of a competition by invitation, because the developers had not yet determined the building density. The four proposals were for a broad, short cone; a medium-sized cylindrical building; and two narrower columns, the second 1,200 feet high. The last would certainly have provided the skyline of London with a new landmark, but in the end all three proposals were refused.

The theme that each solution explores is a development of the handling of office space in the Galeries Lafayette in Berlin. The problem in both projects was how to provide natural daylight to the largest number of offices or rooms, especially those near the center of the building. For the first proposal, a narrow cone similar to the Berlin solution is used. In the second proposal, a circular lightwell in the center is supplemented by a cone that intersects its depth by three-quarters and measures the diameter of the building at the top. In the third and fourth solutions, a narrow lightwell is complemented by three cones, one rising from the third floor and two falling from the roof. Adding cones to lightwells exploits the angular surfaces of the cones to reflect light deeper into the building, thereby extending the daylight exposure even at the lowest levels. This is an elegant technical solution to making office space as lively as possible.

Renderings of the four proposals
for the Baltic Tower: Crystal Dome
(top left), Crystal Wall (top right),
Crystal Tower (bottom left),
Crystal Spire (bottom right)

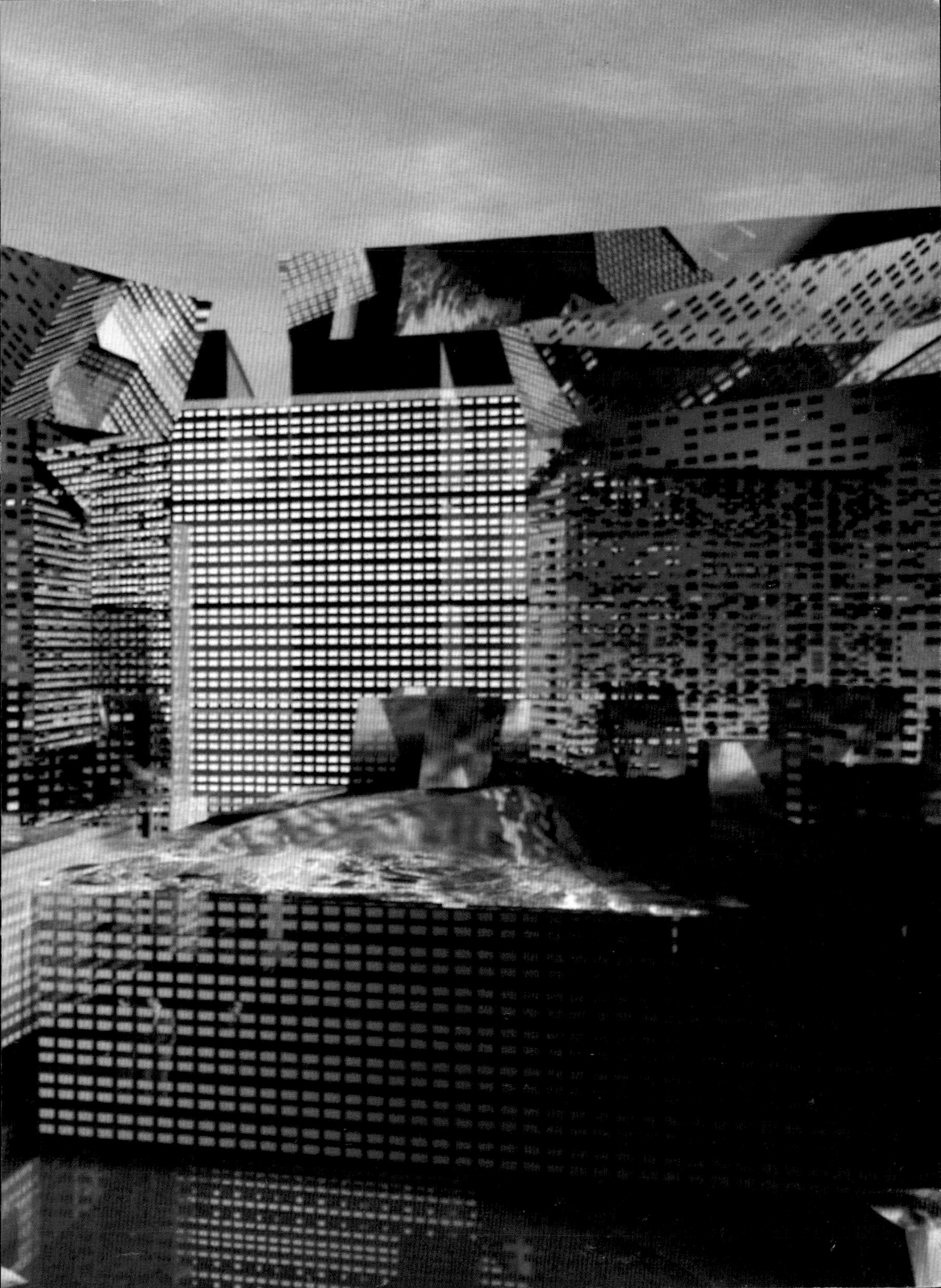

The Fondation Cartier, as the illustrations on these pages show, is a continual evocation of building and context through light and appearance—a central concept in Nouvel's thinking.

# The Importance of Ideas

There are a number of themes that Nouvel's work continually engages. Transparency and presence, function and response, materiality and absence, technology and purpose. His architecture begins in the thought process, in ideas, though not in the sense of applying an ideology or fixed conceptual framework to each project in a modular manner, but through a formal intellectual analysis of the meaning and purpose of each building, its site, and its context.

Nouvel's buildings engage our interest through their consistency of purpose, within the range of their visual or technical complexities. Very often the sequence of impressions one of his buildings creates—from distance to detail, through the arrangement, proportions, and linking of interior elements, in the handling of mass and facade, by the use of color and light—works in a harmonious parallel with the purposes and functions of the building: the qualities of commodity, firmness, and delight cited centuries ago by Vitruvius. But a more modern, and perhaps more appropriate metaphor would be a cinematic one. The framing, duration, and sequencing of the phases of a scene, the handling of contrast and light, the sense of pace and movement—qualities found in film—can also be identified in the statics of Nouvel's buildings.

This cinematic analogy can be taken in several ways with Nouvel's work. In the first place, we know that the cinematic frame is not just an element in the construction of a film sequence, but is itself a medium, a carrier of messages that can be read on a range of levels, and not necessarily through traditional orthographies. For Nouvel, the idea that a building can be a system of signs is an evident one. And, also evidently, the language of such signs is not necessarily only the conventional orthography of architecture, but rather, for a building to survive in its context, to make sense of its place and time, the language must be drawn from all aspects of culture and society, from other media, from anywhere but architecture. Since we live in an increasingly visual culture, the linguistics of the cinema, television, and the world wide web are appropriate to architecture today.

This sign system does not merely relate to the exterior decoration of a building's surfaces (such as the angels proposed for Prague or the Paris cityscape on the Institut du Monde Arabe). Such an application is only one of the layers of meaning concentrated into the totality of a structure, and indeed such a system should itself be multilayered, abstract (the exterior grids at Nantes and Lucerne, for example), and changing (as with the Mediapark and Dumont Schauberg projects). Just as there are many ways of reading a film—through its aesthetics, its dynamics, its use of color or language, its narrative structure, its auteur quality, and so on—so can and should there be many ways of reading a building, of understanding the poetics of its situation. What Nouvel achieves with his buildings is a synthesis between different, possibly contradictory, hypotheses or situations, in a form that is almost always visually exciting and wholly original and yet appropriate for its setting.

The second way in which the cinema metaphor describes Nouvel is in his way of working: he has himself compared the role of the architect to that of a film director. He often assembles a team of experts to work on a project, not only from within the practice, but from a long-standing group of friends, companions who have fought other battles at his side in the past. Others, especially the theater director Jacques Le Marquet, the critic and writer Olivier Boissière, the architect and publisher Hubert Tonka, are what Nouvel calls his sparring partners, on call to discuss his ideas. They and others may be called to advise or discuss a concept, or to take on a specific task, just as a cin-

ema director will chose the lighting cameraman, the art director, and the film editor. But, like the film director, the final choice and ultimate responsibility lie with Nouvel himself, which is why he rightly also describes architecture as a solitary profession. It is the architect who makes the choices, negotiates the changes, organizes the team that delivers the finished building. Nouvel explains:

> At the start of any project there is a series of meetings, discussions, analyses, brainstorming sessions, with the team, with others. Often it can be as simple as making lists—things to do and not to do! That helps me build a mental picture of the possible solutions—and I always remember that architecture is not a matter of single solutions! And then I make a choice—this is a leap into emptiness, like Klein's *Saut dans le vide*, which can be only my choice, the architect's choice, and my responsibility. The choice is a synthesis of the different opportunities and constraints already identified. This I then present to the team as a physical interpretation of the ideas, as a narrative of how this aspect meets this requirement, of why this choice of materials, why this handling of light, and so on. Then we discuss further, and the team starts on drawings and models—which in turn throw up new challenges or contradictions, which we must resolve or adapt to.

This sounds as if the architect zooms in and sees the whole project in one moment of truth: not so. Sometimes the starting point will be a detail, or a particular aspect of the site. I see my first project as a kind of envelope of sensations, built up of requirements and knowledge, emotions and memories, which I feel will work. This doesn't arise from preconceived ideas, but from the project itself. That said, just as a cinema director makes a film to a particular script, he (or she) also makes his or her own personal film; so, also, I create my architecture, and am responsible for its quality, its formal values, its poetics, if you like. And just as the director may go back to the script and amend it, so we will use the original proposal as a reference point, and if need be revise it as the building evolves.

There is a third link: both cinema and architecture depend on light. As Nouvel puts it:

> Traditional architecture was based on fixing solid and void. This approach overlooked the primacy of light, which is what enables us to see architecture at all! And it overlooks the potential of light, and its variability. For me, light is matter, and light is a material, a basic material. Once you understand how light varies, and varies our perceptions, your architectural vocabulary is immediately extended, in ways classical architecture never thought of. An architecture of ephemerality becomes possible—not in the sense of temporary structures, but mutable ones, changed by light and changing with light. Not only through changes in daylight, but through changing the interior lighting of the building, and playing with different opacities and transparencies. Using light effectively is for me a baseline in my architecture. My buildings are planned around five, six, or seven different sets of lighting conditions, from the start. Had I started with just one set—as some other architects still do—the result would be very different: but not acceptable to me!

For Nouvel this question of transparency—of the immateriality of a building—is not just a visual matter. It is also a key factor in what might be termed the presence of a building—the extent and way to which it relates to its site and to its time. This approach takes the modern world's state of

continuous change (at all levels, in all ways) as a starting point, not an irrelevance or a consequence. It responds to ambiguity with ambiguity, to complexities with complexity. The patterns of shadow, space, light, and reflection in the interiors of the Institut du Monde Arabe, for example, are not complex for the sake of being so, but because the definition of the purposes and qualities of the building demanded that level of complexity. The receding glass planes of the Fondation Cartier are not there solely for their astonishing beauty, but also as a necessary mirror and reminder of change and evolution, of time and light. To the static perspectives or orthogonal views of architecture that prevailed in the past, Nouvel prefers an evolving, moving view, a perception that changes with distance, level, and angle, where the storyboard has replaced the drafting board, the video camera has taken over for the easel. He designs with time as well as space and light.

A final aspect of Nouvel's thinking that runs through all of his architecture is the concept of tension—not in the sense of aggression, nor in a Gehryesque sense of gravity, but in a physical sense, as a measure of the state of an object, of its criticality. "What I mean by the term tension is an exact, unambiguous relationship between elements," Nouvel explains, "clear and evident, without illogicality. I'm horrified by buildings that lack tension: they seem soft, unstructured, left to chance not purpose." This is not a matter of leaving structural elements visible, a game Nouvel prefers not to play, but one of logic, of getting the relationship between the elements of the building (and between building and site, building and context) exactly right, maximizing the potential of materials (and so using a minimum of them) but also accepting complexities in a deliberate creation of criticality. And as the scientist Per Bak has pointed out, "complexity is a consequence of criticality."

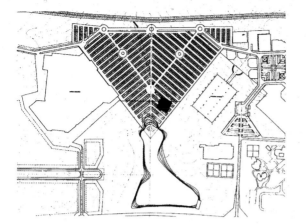

# Onyx Cultural Center

ST. HERBLAIN, FRANCE

The black box is one of the classics of early cybernetics. It derived from the black chamber of the camera, and its most famous incarnation is as the unfortunate location of Schrödinger's cat. The function of a black box is to transform an input and to output the result. Its importance as a concept lies in our not needing to know how the transformation is made in order to use the box.

The Onyx Cultural Center is both metaphor and reality of the black box. Since the building predates cyberspace it could, with hyperbole, be called the first real virtual object. Traditionally theaters and cinemas used, and still use, their architecture to advertise their wares; the peristyle becomes the marquee. In 1987 the town of St. Herblain, near Nantes in western France, held a competition for a cultural center. The brief asked for a 600-seat auditorium, meeting room, and exhibition area. Nouvel won the competition with a black box.

The site for the center was defined by a ten-hectare, triangular parking lot serving a supermarket and a department store. The parking area leads towards a small artificial lake, around which a park was to be created. Thus the site was defined by cars and com-

OPPOSITE View of the building at night

ABOVE Site plan, showing the Onyx building (the small black square) in relation to the parking lot

merce, busy in daylight, dead at night. Nouvel's solution was a perfect half-cube, all black—dead in the daytime, lit at night—set at an angle to the lines of parking spaces, at the apex of the triangle but off-center. The building fits into the slope of the surface, with a low slot of doors opening into the night: part of the parking lot and yet other—a deliberately ambiguous challenge to its context that gains meaning only from its context, for without the vast and artificial space of the parking lot the artifices of the building would have no resonance.

Inside, the main auditorium is finished in corroded galvanized metal plates with grey folding seats. Color is provided by arrays of red lamps under the grey metal lighting gantries that span the hall. The other interior fittings such as ramps and stairways are in flat grey metal with openwork metal treads. The floors are polished concrete, the interior spaces strictly rectilinear, following the defining grid of the exterior. The openwork of the stairs, the job architect Frédérique Monjanel points out, is intended to give clear views across the whole interior and beyond "which we achieved despite the misgivings of the fire department." The spaces are empty of meaning, so forming a counterpoint to the spectacle to be presented within: a necessary neutrality in a multipurpose space.

If the black box is slightly unnerving, there is another, more sinister visual cue that Onyx invokes: that of the bunker, particularly in its relationship to the nearby lake. The complexities and ambiguities of bunkers are now familiar, through Paul Virilio's elegant text *Bunker Archeologie*: "The bunker is the fruit of these lines of force. It is spun from a network under tension with the landscape and through the landscape. . . . The bunker is not really founded: it floats on ground that is not a socle for its balance, but a moving and random expanse that belongs to the ocean expanse, and extends it. It is this relative autonomy that balances the floating bunker, guaranteeing its stability in the middle of probable modifications to the surrounding terrain." Read as a bunker, the entrances and signs become gunports, the corner lights lookout posts, the red markings of the parking lot firing zones, and the external rigid black mesh

OPPOSITE (ABOVE) The auditorium, with the walls covered in steel plates

OPPOSITE (BELOW) In this view of the entrance foyer, one can see the transparency of the interior as compared to the opacity of the exterior.

over the black walls a formal camouflage scrim. This mesh in turn increases the visual density of the building in daylight, masking in part its occasional transparencies formed by windows and doors.

Nouvel's buildings are never single metaphors: a bunker is one reading, the empty anonymous box another. A third is the enigmatic monolith from Stanley Kubrick's film *2001*, as Olivier Boissière suggests. Monjanel reflects on the dynamics of a small box in a large space—"culture in a caddy" as she says. But the building, dark, defined, clear in shape but not purpose, is also a nonobject, which it must be if it is to exist in the nonspace of an immense, anonymous suburban parking lot.

OPPOSITE AND ABOVE Aspects of the black box: the building in relation to the surface signage of the parking lot and bunkered by the artificial lake.

"The railway station at Perpignan is
the center of the universe."

Salvador Dali

# INIST

NANCY, FRANCE

"I imagined that at that very moment he was plunged into his
research work, a hundred leagues away from thinking that in a few
minutes we were going to be once more face to face, a meeting too
often postponed, too, too long desired, too, too, too turbulent. . . ."
This is part of an extract from a novel, *Avis de Recherche*, bought
off the bottom shelf of the railway station bookstall in Perpignan
and reprinted in Olivier Boissière and Georges Fessy's book on the
INIST building. As a piece of romantic fiction, it is too long on
description of the location of this brief encounter and too short on
the emotions and passions of the protagonists. It would seem that
Jean Nouvel, the author, made the right career choice in opting for
architecture. But this literary bagatelle does have more than curios-
ity value, in two respects. First, as we shall see, it highlights one of
the issues underpinning the conception of the building; and second,
the descriptive approach is highly cinematic.

INIST is the headquarters building for the Institut de l'Information
Scientifique et Technique, the French national information institute
for technology and science, part of the CNRS, the national center
for scientific research, one of the French government's main
research institutions. It was decided in the early 1980s, as part of

OPPOSITE The linking corridor to
the main storage unit: the expression of efficiency redeemed by
attention to detail and color

a general policy of decentralization, to move the archives into a new building, away from Paris. The new building, properly equipped for the information age, would be an independent institute. Its purpose would be to store, collate, and distribute scientific information of all kinds and in all media, especially electronic media. A site was chosen near Nancy, in eastern France, and a competition held in 1984, in which Nouvel's project was the unanimous winner.

There is an immediate temptation with such a project to create a science-fiction monolith, all chrome, computer screens, and robots, and plant it in a close encounter with the landscape. But while this could create a beautiful object, it would fail precisely because a beautiful object is all it would be. For Nouvel, thinking of Schopenhauer, any beauty would have to be "the exact representation of efficiency." The meaning of efficiency in this context is not just the storage of information, but the processing of information: raw information comes into one end of the system, and ordered information (digitized, indexed, cross-referenced) comes out of the other. In other words, the building was to be not a storehouse, but an industrial plant; not processing steel or chemicals, but information. Just as the plan and form of a factory is decided by its process, not by aesthetics, so the information-handling process governed the arrangement and relative positions of the units in the scheme. So the central storage unit is linked by a fixed passageway to the main entrance, with the micrographics building and database building feeding into this on one side, the administrative office blocks above micrographics, and social facilities on the other side of the passageway.

OPPOSITE Details of the exterior and stair at INIST

ABOVE General view, showing the micrographics building (foreground), the administration building (left), and the central storage unit (right)

Although industry is one metaphor for the method of arranging the elements in the project, a more appropriate analogy would be the motherboard of a computer, where different elements are linked through their place in the scheme and take on their individual forms in respect of their own functions. So the central storage would equate to the hard disk, the database to the CPU, the micrographics building to the SIMS powering the random access memory, and so on. But the INIST is neither a high-tech factory nor a computer: it is a unique institution, for which the built solution had to be both legible and particular. To have treated all the elements in the same way would not have respected this; equally, to have had too great a mixture of styles would have failed. The architecture is principally in steel, glass, and concrete (contemporary means for contemporary ends), but with differences in the handling that demarcate the individual elements while creating a valid whole in the way that a sequence of shots builds into a film, a coherence of totalities.

Thus the red lines that mark edges of facades and boundaries can be read as directional signs (like the cabalistic markings on airport standings or runways) or demarcation marks (like director's cuts), and the covered passages that link building to building are the tracks and dissolves that move us from scene to scene. It is acceptable to bring this language of motion from the cinema into architecture, because it is a language we all speak and understand, one that is apposite for the twentieth-century condition. So the heroine's progress through the building to find her friend or lover for an uncertain meeting, becomes a long shot: "I walked towards the entrance, past the four cubic steel buildings, in line, trying to see if one of the silhouettes behind the grid of windows on each floor might be his. I turned into the passageway, with its red stripemarks, following a long perspective broken by blue lampholders. The light came from small fittings in the grey, curved ceiling with its formal and relentless grid of perforated metal plates. On each side, a narrow horizontal window showed a slice of the surrounding countryside. As I reached the reception area I found myself strangely fascinated by place dedicated to precision, work and order. . . ."

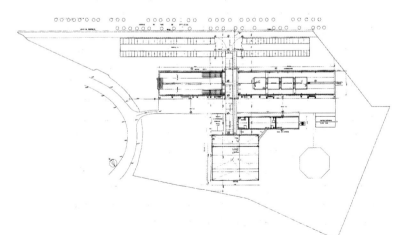

OPPOSITE Roofscapes at INIST showing the links between the different elements on the site

LEFT Site plan

"Travel should not be focussed on architecture alone. It should favor a sensitive perception of a many-sided reality."

Jean Nouvel,
*L'Architecture d'aujourd'hui*, no. 296

# Holiday Homes

CAP D'AIL, FRANCE



Even architects go on holiday. Nouvel, for example, sometimes stays with Jacques Seguela in his house at Sperone in Corsica, designed by Jean-François Bodin (with whom Nouvel worked on an early version of the Fondation Cartier). The invitation to design a group of holiday houses and apartments on the Mediterranean coast of France was therefore a welcome one.

Nouvel's analysis began with the site. It is rocky and steep, almost a cliff, and partly cut into by an old quarry. At the top, pine trees overlook the sea, with a similar seaward view across the whole site. The appropriate architecture would therefore follow the profile of the cliff, almost as an extension of it. "A minimal, mineral architecture," is how Nouvel describes it. The exterior facades are finished in polished stone, matching in color the natural stonework of the cliff. In using a natural material with an artificial surface Nouvel both accepted the dictates of the site and expressed the imposition of the new structure over the original. Another feature of the site plays on the natural/artificial ambiguity: there is a waterfall from the top of the site to the bottom, ending with a cascade of rocks into a large blue swimming pool; the pool has a false horizon on the seaward side so that the blue water of the pool merges almost seamlessly with sky and distant sea.

Detail of the integration of the buildings into the cliff face

ABOVE The Cap d'Ail development
sitting against the cliff above the
village, overlooking the sea


OPPOSITE Sandblasted glass
screens separate balconies

This layered approach to the contextual possibilities of the project is a key to Nouvel's approach to architecture. The constraints of the site become the starting point for a further series of visual and physical allusions (but not illusions) that give the whole development its concrete and individual character. To have built in stone and left it with a natural surface would have been as shallow a response as to have used a wholly artificial material such as concrete. By using stone and cutting and polishing it like concrete Nouvel both affirms the requisites of the site and his own intervention into it.

The apartments were sold as timeshares, so Nouvel was not involved in the interior design beyond the building shell. He did, however, organize the plan so that in most cases it is the long side of the main room that opens on to the balcony, rather than the conventional arrangement of the shorter side. Thus more of the communal living area is open to the sun.

A further aspect of the site validates this approach. At sea level there is an existing row of holiday homes, shops, and restaurants, built to no particular plan, and with the cheerful, indeed slightly vulgar confusion of colors and styles found in most Mediterranean seaside towns. By giving his development a very clear visual appearance, Nouvel separated it from the existing environment.

OPPOSITE The simple stone-faced facades and wooden stairs at Cap d'Ail

ABOVE View from the main street of Cap d'Ail, showing how the development blends into the cliff, following its contours

"A belvedere overlooking the valleyed landscape of the Limousin. It is the home of the Limousin cow and a hymn to the species, the glory of its race, a Western architecture entirely in weathered wood."

Jean Nouvel,
Lecture in Milan, 1995

# Genoscope de Lanaud

LANAUD, FRANCE

The Genoscope de Lanaud stands apart from much of the rest of Jean Nouvel's work. First, it is in a wholly rural context, without even an encircling village, as for the Cartier factory in St. Imier, or an adjoining industrial park, as with the Poulain building in Blois. Second, it is constructed of wood rather than Nouvel's habitual metal and glass. But then the Genoscope is itself some way outside most conventional building types.

The idea for it was conceived by a cattle breeder in the Limousin region of France, Louis de Nerville, whose family have raised cattle in the area for about 450 years. He wished to celebrate and develop the distinctive Limousin breed, and so wanted a building that would house a sale room, a meeting place, a documentation and records center, and a museum, as well as offices for the ten or so independent organizations involved in the Limousin breed. For all this there was a minimal budget, together with a superb site, on the top of a hill overlooking farmland. "The local *directeur d'affaires culturels,* who had earlier been involved with me on the Théatre de Belfort, met de Nerville," Nouvel explains, "who was saying that he didn't think he could interest a major architect in such a minor project, and he sent de Nerville on to see me. We had an interesting

OPPOSITE The sale room at the Genoscope reveals different weathering patterns on the wooden surfaces.

OVERLEAF The office building sits below the brow of the hill (left), with the belvedere and sale room to the right.

19 | 20

discussion—architecture was not his field, he simply wanted the best for his project, and at first he didn't understand what we were trying to do. Once he did—which was rapidly—his support was enthusiastic."

Nouvel's decision to build in wood was partly dictated by the budget, since there was a good local source for Douglas fir, and partly because wood was a logical material for farm building. However, as Edouard Boucher, the job architect, points out, "wood isn't a peasant material, so to speak. Peasants and farmers want solidity and permanence, so build in stone when they can. But there is a good rural tradition of building with the materials that are to hand, and of using wood for barns and stables."

The form of the buildings was decided in part by the site, in part by its different functions. The site is on the brow of a gentle hill, offering broad vistas over the surrounding countryside under immense skies. This in itself suggested horizontality, a profile that would mark the skyline without dominating it. One building, triangular in section, contains the offices on two levels under the sloping roof. The elevation is a long rectangular wall of narrow horizontal slats, pierced with unrecessed window and door openings. The main building, set at an angle to the offices and a short distance away, makes use of the ground slope. Viewed from the south, there is a single story to the left, containing the restaurant and museum area. This opens onto an immense deck above the sale room. The deck, laid in an angled checkerboard pattern of wooden slats, offers broad views across the surrounding countryside. "What I like about the building is its naturalness," says Nouvel, "so because of the weathering of the wood, it seems to fit into the landscape, yet it isn't quite like anything else there: it's slightly out of the frame. You don't quite know how long it has been there." It appears both familiar and unfamiliar—wooden architecture, for cattle, seemingly transposed from the Hollywood Western screen to the pastures of France, and formal, rectilinear shapes introduced into a natural landscape. It is these layers of superimposition, different but relevant cultural references stacked into a very simple building, that make the Genoscope so interesting, a minor element in Nouvel's oeuvre, but sharing with greater projects the same depth of vision and precision.

Bulls for auction being driven into the sale room at the Genoscope

# Furniture Design

Architects are always designing furniture—it is one of the accepted aspects of contemporary design. Wright did it, Le Corbusier did it, Mies did it. The motives are various: Wright was quite insistent that his clients accept his furniture designs for their private houses, leading one client to name a particular armchair after a famous boxer: "It's as hard to sit in it as it is to hit him," he wrote to Wright. For Le Corbusier, it was perhaps more a question of showing a multiplicity of talents—writer, architect, painter, designer had a nice Renaissance ring to it. For Mies, many of his designs were intended for specific locations, most famously the Barcelona Pavilion. Many young architects also design furniture to try out concepts that they have not had the opportunity to build full-scale.

Nouvel's furniture design includes such youthful work, such as a set of boxes of decreasing size that hang from rails in the ceiling along which they can be moved. It is an elegant, space-saving solution, though wholly architectural. As one furniture designer said when I showed him the design, "It must be by an architect. Everyone else starts from the floor up!" The design is wholly an exercise in space and proportion, and was commissioned by VIA, a body set up by the French Ministry of Culture to promote French furniture design. The

OPPOSITE The Touch collection

TTL table is in the same series, a solid construction in matte aluminum that can be raised and lowered using a hydraulic piston incorporated into the base. These two pieces can be read as deliberate attempts to explore industrial forms in a domestic or office setting. They were included in an exhibition entitled "Les Cartes Blanches VIA," together with a folding table and the toolbox of memories "Coffre BAO" in 1987.

After these *exercices de style*, Nouvel came back to furniture design two years later, first with his seating design for the Lyon Opera House, a black aluminum frame supporting a rounded plastic back and folding seat, incorporating a fiber-optic lamp. Over 1,300 of these were made for the new Opera House, but the design was, not surprisingly, never manufactured commercially. Far more important was the series of chairs, tables, beds, and cabinets Nouvel designed for the Hôtel St. James. While these simple but engaging curved forms with plain cushioning were specifically designed for the hotel, they had sufficient individual validity to be taken up commercially by French furniture makers Ligne Roset, who made them available commercially in 1990, and in 1991 also launched a new sofa and armchair by Nouvel.

Nouvel called the design *Elementaire*, and he described its conception and design in the 1995 *International Design Yearbook*: "It's about what I call basics, elementary things. The degree zero of design. *Elementaire* is a black armchair, dumb, cubic, minimal. It's well made but it's nothing else. 'Move on, there's nothing to see here,' it says. It's the kind of furniture I need because I've no time for furniture caricatures that dislocate and travesty the meaning of a place. Let me make this clear: I hate all furniture as fashion, created like styles, overdone, over-referential. I need simple things, so I set about making simple things. Anti-design, free of imagination. *Elementaire* is black and square, it works ergonomically. It's neither very comfortable nor very uncomfortable. It's normal. And Roset simply said, 'Done,' when they saw it." And, it must be said, when Ligne Roset did it, Nouvel furnished his flat in Paris—at the time just opposite the Pompidou Center—with it.

OPPOSITE Two pieces of aluminum furniture produced as prototypes for VIA in 1987: a variable-height table (above) and a set of hanging, movable shelves (below)

Nouvel's next project involving furniture was the CLM/BBDO build-ing in Issy-les-Moulineaux. He designed a rolltop desk, a compro-mise between a traveling salesperson's case and a fixed object, fol-lowing Philippe Michel's dictum that salespeople were nomads, and his deeper, unstated understanding that salespeople are loners and want to keep their business to themselves until the right moment. His other design for CLM/BBDO was a fat, armless armchair in red leather with a broad back, so that you could sit on it (from the front) or lean on it (at the back). I first saw it in Nouvel's office. "You can use either side of it," he explained.

Nouvel's other main furniture project in 1993–94 was for the Fon-dation Cartier, comprising desk and storage systems in grey lac-quered steel. A desk, said Nouvel, is only a supported surface. So the Cartier desk (called LSS, as Nouvel dislikes vowels) is a minimal surface on narrow legs. The skill of the design lies in the way the steel surface has been reinforced so as to maintain its rigidity as well as its narrow profile. The elegance of the solution derives from its simplicity; the same is true for the storage units, which are care-fully proportioned boxes on swivelling stands. The overall aim of both is that within the Cartier building no furniture of any sort would be pushed against the windows, thus maintaining the evanes-cence of the structure. The function of the furniture has been reduced to essentials, and the suite evolved from there. One Cartier employee I met inspecting his future office at the opening of the Fondation called the furniture "pure Tati," comparing his new work-place with the wit and charm of the modern interiors in Tati's film Mon Oncle, in which modern gadgets are taken to extremes. He was delighted; only in France would an employee think that a forty-plus-year-old film was an appropriate metaphor for his future workplace.

Nouvel liked the comparison: "A minimal solution to a space gives room for personality. LSS was designed to match the building, so it is visually discreet, and in particular it was created so that there would be no furniture against the walls. But if you look at the build-ing now, some years on, you can see how the office spaces have become individual. I hate the idea of the formal office, measured out in millimeters and with fixed furnishings." The designs are now mar-

keted by Unifor under the generic title Less. As Nouvel says about the chair he has designed to accompany Less, "Working with elementary forms has a natural logic within my approach to architecture, but in addition I believe that furniture should not impose itself on a space. It should help to articulate the space, not dominate it. There should be a certain reserve about furniture, to allow the owner to express himself or herself around it."

In addition to these designs related to specific buildings, Nouvel has also been involved in creating individual designs, particularly for Sawaya and Moroni in Milan, a company with a strong commitment to innovation. Nouvel's Milana chair plays deliberate games with Mies van der Rohe's Barcelona chair. "Suppose you pulled its leg!" Nouvel explained in the 1995 *Design Yearbook*. This is what he did, twisting the legs, rather than extending them. The result is neither absurd nor fanciful; it is both a restatement of the dynamic tension in the original chair, and a new object, lively and nervous in its own right. Putting the idea of the Barcelona chair to the test has wrought from it a new definition. As in Nouvel's architecture, new definitions continually emerge.

Another major project for an independent editor is a desk-workstation, designed for and marketed by Bulo in Belgium under the name Quasi Normal. Bulo's original invitation was to design the desk Nouvel would most like to have in his own office. Since Nouvel has no office, preferring to move from desk to desk or use communal spaces, this was something of a problem. The resulting design is personable rather that personal, consisting of a flat plane under or upon which various objects, such as filing cabinets or monitor screens, could be placed. It is an essentially simple object, but one capable of complexity: the elements under the desk could rotate through 360 degrees, so that the whole could be a desk for one person or two; it could become a long unit or a short one; and so on. When I first saw

OPPOSITE AND BELOW The Elementaire armchair and sofa, commissioned by Ligne Roset and designed by Nouvel to be simple, anonymous, and comfortable

it, set up as a single desk, it reminded me of a monk's cell—not for its austerity, direct though it is, but for its sense of completeness and concentration.

Nouvel designed a more grandiose project for Mobilier International under the title Box Office. If Less was minimalist and Quasi Normal generalist, Box Office is blatantly about power. It is intended as a complete working environment for a company president or CEO, with installed units for monitors, computer hardware, phones and fax, cigarette lighter and ashtray, all hidden within a massive black slab. This is a metaphor that has been explored before, notably in de Lucchi and Castiglioni's elegant San Girolamo desk and shelving system, a design that really puts power into the power office. Nouvel's black box (literally, in that only the user knows which features are hidden where) is a physical statement of the abstraction of his own design process. He himself doesn't have one in his office, because he doesn't have an office.

With the creation of Architectures Jean Nouvel, the design side was at first put into a separate business, JND (Jean Nouvel Design) but has since been absorbed into the main enterprise. The design group is now working on a number of lighting projects, ceramic tableware, and, appropriately, a series of tables incorporating a fixed tablecloth for bars and restaurants at the KKL building in Lucerne.

At the 1998 Salone del Mobile in Milan, Nouvel unveiled a number of new pieces, as either prototypes or finished products. These included a new series of stools, high and low chairs, and a table for Poltrona Frau called Touch. "I wanted to get away from the tyranny of the visual," Nouvel explained, "and invest instead in tactile qualities. The sensuous, almost muscular feel of leather is ideal for this." The seating consists of simple, round pads mounted on X-frame supports and covered in black leather. The leather has a plain, even surface, with no lines or seams, and in pursuit of a tactile goal, their visual appearance has an almost deliberate frailty.

Other projects included a series of storage units for home or office, based on a modular cube, from Kartell; a panel lamp for Luce Plan;

The furniture for the CLM/BBDO building consisted of a consultant's desk that folds like a carrying case and broad-backed red leather armchairs for spontaneous meetings (opposite) a wall-mounted lightbox, up to two meters wide, that backlights a changeable scroll of images.

The most interesting collection shown was the new LSS chairs and horizontal storage units, from Unifor. These complement the LSS tables and vertical storage systems devised for the Cartier building. The storage units, mounted on A-frame supports, repeat the box motif of their vertical cousins and can be stacked up to three deep, with doors that open either up or down according to the position of the unit.

The LSS chair rigorously follows the logics of the LSS tables: narrow, square-profile legs, a minimal seat platform, and severely rectangular seat and back cushions in foam. The back is supported by a hinged internal metal panel that allows two positions. This variable angle and the comfort of the seating deliberately contradict the severity of the chair's appearance. The chair, together with a mobile computer support unit exhibited at Milan in 1997, completes the LSS line. The computer furniture is a series of computer-sized trays on casters, designed to fit at the back or the side of a LSS table.

The LSS designs act as an elegant summary of Nouvel's attitude toward design, "something quite separate from architecture," as he once said, but related to his perceptions of context's and society's roles in creative work. The designs show both a desire to maximize technology in the search for a visual solution and a desire for non-interference by the designer in the way the final product is used. Thus the collection is both a personal statement and a democratic one, reflecting the two levels of decision Nouvel refers to in his approach to architectural projects.

The LSS table and vertical storage
unit designed for the Fondation
Cartier and marketed by Unifor. A
chair, computer table, and horizontal storage unit have been added to
the line.

# As to the Future

"The skyscraper and the twentieth century are synonymous: the tall building is the landmark of our age," Ada Louise Huxtable wrote in *The Tall Building Artistically Reconsidered*. "... From the Tower of Babel onward, the fantasies of builders have been vertical rather than horizontal." With the end of the century approaching, Nouvel, too, is considering a skyscraper, though not fantastically. It is a project for the Dentsu Corporation, for a site overlooking Tokyo Bay. The plans are due to be unveiled in fall 1998, after the publication of this book.

The need to redefine the concept of the skyscraper as a human building, as an integral construction rather than an imposed one, has already been faced by Nouvel in his projected designs for the Tour Sans Fins and for the Baltic Tower in London. One aspect studied particularly in these two projects was a means of bringing natural light into the interior of the building and creating—especially in the Tour Sans Fins—uncluttered floor space on all levels. The architect's proposed solutions in each case were different, not because Nouvel is eclectic, or always seeking novelty, but because different situations demand different responses. With the Dentsu project, the splendor of the site, its physical and cultural location, evokes a very specific response, but one that also addresses the wider issues of making tall buildings that have a human scale and character.

Nouvel once defined the secret aim of the architect as being the desire to convey pleasure and to embellish everyday life. This is achieved through exploring a series of hypotheses about a particular project and its context, its purpose and function in human, cultural, political, and geographical terms. The concept once defined creates a certain number of perceptions—visual, sensual, or verbal—which, in Nouvel's words, "reveal and tame the genus loci" and so can be turned from the abstract into the concrete, a system of signs and meanings that is both specific to the place and universal in its essence, able to communicate to all. The concrete reality must be achieved through moderation, with a minimum of interference (which requires that technology be used both unobtrusively and with maximum accuracy and application), and with harmony, not only between the parts that make up the whole, but also between the whole and its surroundings, both spatially and temporally.

"The future of architecture is not Architectural," Nouvel has said. It is a suitably complex and contradictory comment, with several layers of meaning. It does not mean that architecture has no future; rather, that architecture has no past, in the sense that architecture can no longer conceive of itself as an independent discipline, bound only by its own rules. This is because the modern social and urban context is too complex for a single set of rules to be valid. Neither the historical rules of architecture nor the modern ones, in Nouvel's view, offer a feasible starting point. "We cannot create buildings for the future," he explains, "only from a knowledge of architectural history. The technical and cultural revolutions and evolutions of the twentieth century have seen to that. Similarly I find the design of ideal buildings or ideal city plans quite absurd; more than that, a totalitarian aberration. The idea that we can impose ideological rules is wrong in itself, and is wholly inappropriate for building in the modern city, where there are no rule structures any more." There was a time when the architectural statement was the grammar of urbanism, the logics of civil society or religious order literally set in stone. The multiple foci of modern living, the relentless flow of information, imagery, and material goods—traffic in the widest sense of the word—have created a situation in which such a singular vision is no longer possible. The nature of architectural intervention has changed radically, and been altered by outside forces. This does not mean that the architect can do nothing, nor does it mean that the architect

One vision of the future is to be found in Nouvel's proposal's, illustrated here and on the following two pages, for major exhibitions he is involved in creating for the Hanover 2000 exhibition in Germany. The themes of "mobility" and the "future of work" are explored through interactive environments animated with moving images and changing spatial volumes.

can do anything he or she wishes; it is neither a precept for incapacity nor self-indulgence.

It is, instead, a situation, according to Nouvel, that imposes on the architect the dual duties of sensitivity and honesty: sensitivity in the specificity of the project itself—a building is to be created at a specific place, for specific purposes, in a specific context, and sensitivity in a wider, cultural sense. For if the rules of architecture no longer validate the act of architecture, the architect must look elsewhere. In Nouvel's view it is contemporary culture, with its richness and diversity, to which the architect should turn. In an interview with *El Croquis* in 1994 he summarized the position thus:

> Architectural questions arise from the comprehension and enjoyment of the world around us, rather than from the enclosure

within the discipline. Le Corbusier was the first to reveal the potential of the observation of other processes of production when applied to architecture: grain silos, ocean liners, planes.... Virilio has also revealed this extraordinary substratum that armament is as a field of research in the processes of formalization. It is true, there is nothing as beautiful as a weapon.... The military world is a premonitory world because it enjoys the most powerful technological and financial means: every invention has already gone through the military. Nobody can deny the power of seduction of a F-1 car or a racing motorbike ... What is being exhibited currently in New York are Ferraris.... When I affirm that modernity is still alive it is because I understand that it is always a phenomenon of perpetual emergence, not an historical movement. To be

modern is not to be Corbusian, but to have a sensitive attitude to all phenomena of emergence! And this emergence is transversal; it operates through exteriority.

Honesty also has two senses: It stands for absolute clarity in the analysis of the preconditions and parameters of a project, a refusal to discard what is inconvenient, to adapt an existing solution rather than create an original one. It also is the sense of taking responsibility for the architectural act, for its creativity, for the visions and decisions, memories and necessities it incarnates. "Architecture must be absolutely truthful." Nouvel wrote in *L'Architecture d'aujourd'hui* in 1994:

> Being authentic (authentic, defined as what derives from the profound nature of a person) is being

ready to be always on the alert, ready to listen to the lessons of history, to work to put to rights a culture continually under threat in details and in fundamentals. It is about destroying and eradicating errors, "at the coalface," becoming part of what Bachelard termed "the union of workers for proof," being ready to take the role of "the specific intellectual. . . ." Being authentic involves unmasking and denouncing the serious failures of sensitivity in almost all contemporary construction and planning, which lack art and lack pleasure, and can only have been started by people lacking in desire! As a consequence, authenticity is about being ready to disturb (in the emotional sense of the term), to communicate desire—a real desire, as opposed to a duplicated one—stemming from conscience of the *genus hominum* and the *genus loci*. . . . Being authentic is finally about refusing to follow the

flow of cultural stereotypes, about refusing to copy (so as instead to create), refusing to follow (so as to follow one's own path). Already we are busy trying to improve failed buildings too rapidly built. These are false sites, without soul, without charm, without warmth, without knowledge. What will transcend them is conviction, sincerity, willpower, and a love of life.

In my personal view, what makes Jean Nouvel's work as an architect so compelling and so relevant for the contemporary condition of architecture is its authenticity: the direct confrontation between culture and society and site; the analytical process that precedes the creation of designs—in particular its scope. Nouvel's architecture is an architecture of ideas, the fruit of a continuous, informed meditation on the contemporary condition of the city and its inhabitants, which I find both satisfying for its intellectual logic and correct for the state of the world today. There are other approaches to architecture that show vision and inspiration, which can produce exciting results, and there are plenty of able thinkers in the ranks of architects, but few have Nouvel's particular intellectual qualities or his perception that architecture alone is not enough. Nouvel admits that to create any project "there has to be a creative leap, once all the data has been gathered and sorted, the limits and priorities analyzed and discussed." That leap has to be the architect's alone, but it has—afterwards—to be validated by the logic of the project. In other words, if the moment of architecture, when the mass of ideas, reflections, and verbal concepts takes a visible form, is, like Yves Klein's *Saut dans le vide*, impossible to fix or define but does demonstrably exist, it is, for Nouvel, a leap from terra firma, from a fixed and defined point. He mistrusts architecture based only on inner visions—while sometimes admiring the results—because it cannot be analyzed. But at the same time the process is not wholly analytical. He quotes the singer Claude Nougaro: "On the black screen of my white (sleepless) nights, I make my own cinema." He admits he does most of his best thinking in bed ("I think that's true for a lot of other people," he adds with a laugh, "only they don't admit to it.") Because Nouvel "dreams with his eyes open," as T.E. Lawrence put it, he is able to make his dreams a reality. And the realities he creates catch our interest because we know that beyond the structured idea of each building, satisfying intellectually in itself, there is a wider and deeper mass of references with which we can engage.

Furthermore, an attitude of engagement, both with personal sensibilities and real, social, and human issues, is, in my own view, the only possible stance for the architect today. The idea of the architect-creator as the solitary, creative visionary is as false, out-of-date, irrelevant, and dishonest as the bourgeois nineteenth century that created it. Architecture is no longer an independent act; it is one event in a changing continuum of contexts, a durable event that places an additional responsibility on the architect (unlike, for example, such creators of intentional ephemera such as the graphic designer, or, indeed, the architectural writer). The concept of context here is not limited to the immediate landscape nor some set of "rules of architecture," both of which are frames either too narrow or irrelevant. Strategies of urbanism have not been able to dominate the urban context either: we can regard the recent failures of postwar urbanism—the demolished tower blocks, the polluting motorways, the recreation of the ghetto, the anomie of the street—as heroic or absurd, according to taste. But we must accept that their failure was implicit in their beginning, their vision too narrow from the start. They did not understand that the city was driven by forces which planning could not plan or control, even in the past. We have to take the actual state of the city, in as much as we can grasp its Heraclitan fluidity, as a starting point, and develop strategies for guiding and understanding its evolution. From this standpoint, cloning the past is no way to read the genome of the future.

# Suggested Reading

For a fuller understanding of Nouvel's work, the reader is advised to consult the following:

Boissière, Olivier. *Jean Nouvel* (Terrail, 1996).

Boissière, Olivier. *Jean Nouvel* (Artemis/Birkhauser, 1994).

Goulet, Patrice. *Jean Nouvel* (Editions du Regard, 1994).

Nouvel, Jean. *Architecture and Design 1976–1995* (Skira, 1997).

Zaera, Alejandro. *Jean Nouvel 1987–1994* (*El Croquis*, no. 65/66, 1995).


Other books consulted or quoted by the author include:

Bak, Per. *How Nature Works* (Oxford University Press, 1997).

Boissière, Olivier. *L'Inist dans l'oeuvre de Jean Nouvel* (Editions du Demi-Cercle, 1992).

Huxtable, Ada Louise. *The Tall Building Artistically Reconsidered* (Pantheon Books, 1994).

Koolhaas, Rem, and Bruce Mau. *S,M,L,XL* (Monacelli Press/Taschen, 1994).

Nouvel, Jean. *International Design Yearbook 1995* (Laurence King, 1995).

*Poetics/Politics* (Cantz, 1997).

Rice, Peter. *An Engineer Imagines* (Artemis, 1994).

Tanizaki, Junichiro. *Eloge de l'Ombre* (POF, 1993).

Tonka, Hubert. *Opera de Tokyo* (Editions du Demi-Cercle, 1989).

Virilio, Paul. *Bunker Archeologie* (CIC, 1975).

Virilio, Paul. *Esthétique de la Disparition* (Balland, 1980).

Wenders, Wim. *The Logic of Images* (Faber, 1991).

# Captions to Photo Sections

LIGHT

**8–9** Light and color: view of the housing units at Euralille

**10–11** Light and layers: view of Chateaubriand's Tree of Liberty through the office dividers and exterior glazing of the Fondation Cartier

**12** Light and grid: office space at the Cartier factory in St. Imier, Switzerland, designed by Nouvel in 1989

**13** Interior and exterior: entrance passageway at the St. Poulain factory, Blois, France, designed by Nouvel in 1989

**14–15** The building as sign system: model for the Mediapark building in Cologne, Germany, 1991

**16–17** Light and surface: polished plaster walls in the Hôtel St. James, Bouliac

COLOR

**78–79** Color and industrial form: housing units in the Nemausus building, Nîmes

**80–81** Color and line: external wall detailing at the Theatre de Belfort, France (left), and in an exhibition for the Milan Salone, designed with the assistance of Anne Fremy

**82–83** Color as enrichment: housing at Bezons, France, 1994

**84–85** Color as disguise: the Lycée Dhouda in Nîmes was damaged by fire, and Nouvel was asked to advise on redecoration. With the artist Alain Bonny, he selected a repertory of interventions based on the work—in which fire, gold, and blue featured so prominently—of Yves Klein

GRIDS

**168–69** Grids and exteriors: the facade of the Hôtel St. James, Bouliac

**170–71** Grids and light: freestanding wall at the St. Poulain factory, Blois, France

**172–73** Grids and space: glass blocks at Maison Cognacq-Jay, Reuil (left), and the public areas in the Da Vinci Center, Tours

**174–75** Grids and buildings: competition proposal for rehabilitating an office building in Basel, Switzerland, 1998

DETAILS

**218** Detail as enlargement: Egyptian exhibition at the Institut du Monde Arabe, Paris, designed by Nouvel

**219** Detail and light: the gilding at the Lyon Opera House reflected in the polished granite floor

**220** Detail and message: external wall decoration at the projected DuMont Schauberg building, Cologne, Germany, 1990

**221** Detail and grid: the Fondation Cognacq-Jay, Malmaison

**222–23** Detail and volume: light and grids at the Hôtel Les Thermes, Dax, France, designed by Nouvel in 1990

**224–25** Detail and surface: a range of surface textures used at the INIST building, Nancy

# Photography & Project Credits

All computer plans, drawings, models, and computer-generated images are © copyright Architectures Jean Nouvel.

All photographs are by Philippe Ruault, except as follows:
Georges Fessy, **100–103**, **190**
Gaston Bergeret, **14**, **16**, **18**, **99**
Olivier Boissière, **117**, **168**
Christian Demontfaucon, **219**
G. Fox, **120**

The following is a list of Nouvel's principal collaborators on the projects, buildings, and competitions discussed in this book.

Jean Nouvel, François Seigneur, Roland Baltéra: Delbigot House.

Jean Nouvel, François Seigneur, Gilbert Lézénès: School at Tresillac, France.

Jean Nouvel, Gilbert Lézénès, Dominique Tissier: Clinic at Bezons, France.

Jean Nouvel, Gilbert Lézénès: Collège Anne Franck and Les Godets, Antony, France.

Jean Nouvel, Gilbert Lézénès, Dominique Lyon: Theatre de Belfort, France.

Jean Nouvel, Gilbert Lézénès, Patrick Colombier: Gymnasium, Luzard, France.

Jean Nouvel, Gilbert Lézénès, Pierre Soria: La Coupole Cultural Center, Ministère des Finances, Paris.

Jean Nouvel, Gilbert Lézénès, Pierre Soria, Architecture Studio: Institut du Monde Arabe, Paris.

Jean Nouvel, Pierre Soria, Jean-Marc Ibos, Didier Laroque, Architecture Studio: Téte-Défense, Paris.

Jean Nouvel, Jean-Marc Ibos: Médiathèque, Nîmes.

Jean Nouvel, Jean-Marc Ibos, Frédéric Chambon, Jean-Rémi Negre: Nemausus, Nîmes.

Jean Nouvel et Associés, Philippe Starck, as part of the Ateliers de Nîmes: Tokyo Opera House.

Jean Nouvel as part of the Ateliers de Nîmes: Lycée Dhouda, Nîmes.

Jean Nouvel et Associés: INIST, Nancy (Jean-François Guyot, Hossein Hedayati); Lyon Opera House (Emmanuel Blamont); Onyx Cultural Center, St. Herblain (Myrto Vitart); Tour Sans Fins, Paris.

Jean Nouvel and subsequently JNEC (Jean Nouvel and Emmanuel Cattani): CLM/BBDO, Paris; Poulain Factory, Blois; Housing, Bezons; da Vinci Center, Tours; KKL, Lucerne, first project; DuMont Schauberg, Cologne; Cartier Factory, St. Imier, Switzerland; Hôtel Les Thermes, Dax, France; Media park, Cologne; Fondation Cartier, Paris; Galeries Lafayette, Berlin; Schmikov Quarter, Prague; Seine Rive Gauche, Paris; Cité Justiciaire, Nantes.

JNEC and Edouard Boucher: Genoscope de Lanaud.

JNEC with Paindavoine & Associates: Euralille, Lille.

Architectures Jean Nouvel: KKL, Lucerne, second project; Fondation Cognacq-Jay, Rueil; Tenaga Nasional, Kuala Lumpur; Andel building and ING offices, Prague; Baltic Tower, London.

# Index